Divorce, Now What?!

How to Survive, Thrive and Become Truly

Alive Through the Divorce Process

Anne-Louise DePalo Esq.

INTRODUCTION
"Do you want to be made whole?" - John 5:6

Divorce. The word brings fear and trepidation to anyone that it leaves in its wake. The first question to ask yourself when you know that divorce is inevitable is "What now?" Yes, divorce is one of the most difficult and painful experiences anyone can go through. My heart breaks for you. It is a painful and difficult process. Not only is it one of the most stressful events that someone can experience during their lifetime, but it is also akin to experiencing a death: the death of a marriage. It causes emotional wounds and trauma that require healing and care. Carl Jung, the famous Swiss psychiatrist who founded analytical psychology, said that the most traumatic psychological events occur in and around the ending of relationships.

Divorce, with its specter of betrayal, abandonment, disappointment, and dashed hopes, is one of the greatest traumas

2

anyone can face. A relationship is irretrievably broken; hurt and pain follow. It is a death. During divorce, there is a time to grieve. However, when you are thrown into this situation unexpectedly, it is impossible to take the time that you need to grieve. There is so much to do: seek an attorney, attend conferences, meetings or court appearances with your attorney, and care for yourself and your children. All this while trying to see your way clearly.

Nonetheless, when something dies, something new can be born again. I wrote this book to help you, not only through the process legally and financially, but also to support you emotionally, physically and spiritually. It is a step-by-step guide to self-determination and transformation. Often, after trauma, a new life can begin again. You can grow deeper emotionally, intellectually, physically, and spiritually. You can discover your true self. You can survive, thrive, and become truly alive!

In the pages of this book, I will be your guide on every aspect of divorce. Divorce is described in Wikipedia as "dissolution of marriage or marital union, the canceling or reorganizing of the legal duties and responsibilities of marriage, thus dissolving the bonds of matrimony between a married couple under the rule of law of the particular country or state. The issue of alimony (spouse support) child custody, visitation, property distribution, parenting access, medical coverage, life insurance, are determined by the court."

Divorce is distinguished from "annulment," which means a marriage is declared void; that is, it never happened due to reason such as fraud, lack of capacity, etc. This process varies state to state. Legal separation is different from divorce in that spouses outline their legal obligation and responsibilities in a formal contract but remain legally married.

Many spouses are confused by the difference between "physical" separation and "legal" separation. While spouses may live separately for days, months, or even years, they remain married until there is a formal divorce or a signed and acknowledged legal separation.

There are a number of processes by which one can be divorced. I will explain each one in detail in this book, but I will give a brief description here. There is a contested divorce, whereby the parties seek court intervention. Mediation is when both spouses seek an independent, trained mediator to negotiate terms of the divorce. A mediator is neutral and does not advocate for either spouse. Collaborative divorce is when both spouses are represented by collaboratively-trained attorneys. Collaborative law is a form of alternative dispute resolution, where spouses and their lawyers pledge not to go to court. It stresses cooperation rather than confrontation and uses problem-solving and shared interests to resolve the issues involved in the divorce.

Through my experience as a family lawyer for over thirty years, I will give you priceless advice and steps to follow. I am an expert in the legal process of divorce an experienced litigator. I am also a trained collaborative attorney, a certified mediator, a certified parent coordinator, and a certified spiritual director.

Most importantly, I have also been through divorce myself. Although no two divorce experiences are the same, I can relate to what you are going through. I have been divorced twice. Both divorces were painful; however, they helped my transformation. I learned the hard way there are not always happy endings, like in fairy tales, but both endings lead me to immense growth and serenity. The first divorce taught me how to live alone, got me into therapy, and forced me to redefine and focus on my goals; but my growth stopped there. I did not connect the mind, psyche, and spirit. The second divorce led me to Al-anon, psychotherapy, and a deep searching for the meaning of life. I wanted more out of life, and I was opened to the spirit. I finally realized what was missing, and I learned how to care for myself physically, mentally, emotionally, and spiritually. I began a journey, which I am still on. I invite you to join me on this incredible journey. My wish for you is to get it right the first time. This time.

As a parent coordinator and also having represented children in divorce as their assigned attorney, I see the trauma that divorce can cause children. Parents who do not know how to co-parent and navigate through the judicial process and the separation of the family cannot protect their children and ensure that their children are raised as they intended. I will also help you manage your expectations and give you the knowledge and power to make that happen.

You must be educated as to the legal process. I know this sounds like a lot of new information and may seem overwhelming at times, but I am here to help make it easier for you. I will break it down step-by-step. You also need to understand your finances so that you can endure the divorce financially. You must be savvy and take an interest in your financial future, and make it a top priority. A divorce can financially devastate you and your children. I will give you the tools and guide you in this process so that you are prepared and do not make the common financial mistakes that many do during a divorce.

You must know how to care for yourself during your divorce. Think of the process of a caterpillar becoming a butterfly. The caterpillar becomes "pupa" known as a cocoon or (chrysalis) for a butterfly. The caterpillar becomes a cocoon so that it can be nourished, rest, and grow. Then it can break free and emerge as the butterfly and fly free. To grow you must care for yourself physically, mentally, emotionally, and spiritually. Think of the divorce as being in a cocoon. Your former life you were a caterpillar.

You also need knowledge about the legal process, finances, and judicial system. I will be your coach, your educator, and guide you to make proper choices. You will have the answer to "now what?" The "D-word" does not have to be one of death, of destruction. It can also be a new beginning. I tell all my clients that the process itself is extremely difficult; however, when it is over, you will be closing one book and beginning a new chapter. This new book of your life is what you must focus on, and you need to prepare yourself in all aspects so that you can write your own destiny.

I recite this quote from Anthony De Mello often. It says so much so perfectly: "Say goodbye to golden yesterdays, or your heart will never learn to love the present already gone. We live out our lives in chains not knowing we have the keys."

I will pave the way for you to become physically and emotionally healthy and spiritually healed, as you move through your divorce. Divorce is a catalyst that touches all aspects of your life: your health, stress level, time, finances, family, children, social life, emotions, energy, and spirit all are affected and turned upside down. Take heart. It can be turned right side up. All you need to do is be open and committed. If you listen, do what I suggest, and prepare, as I instruct you, you will emerge from the cocoon and emerge as the butterfly you were meant to be. Fly with me.

CHAPTER 1 - THE LEGAL PROCESS

"There's nothing more calming in difficult moments than knowing there's someone fighting for you." - Saint Teresa of Calcutta.

There are a number of ways to divorce. It is best to educate yourself on these different legal processes prior to filing for divorce. Any attorney that you consult with should speak with you about the different processes available. Let me introduce you to Martha. Martha came into my office at the urging of her best friend, Meg, who was a former client. Martha had seen another attorney, a male litigator who advertised as guaranteeing "aggressive" representation. His trademark was a picture of a Pitbull. Martha was frightened, devastated, and very angry by her husband's infidelity, and, in her current state of despair and confusion, she made a rash and hasty decision based on her emotion. She told me her attorney took a very large retainer and promised her the world. He did not explain the law, the different ways to divorce, the possible outcomes, and he gave her no emotional support. If she asked a question, he said he would take care of it and knew what was best. Not much had been done in three months, and she and her husband were not speaking, though they lived in the same house. Her children were being affected. She was not sleeping and was unable to focus at work. When I asked what she wanted she simply said, "I don't know." Then she began to cry.

After sitting with me she told me she got more out of our meeting about the process, the law, and what to expect than from her own attorney in the three months since she retained him. She told me she felt comfortable, listened to, and felt as if I cared about her. She thanked me for my honesty and asked me to take over her case. The case was resolved a few months later. Martha took my advice and was sleeping, eating better, seeing a therapist, and able to care for herself and her children. If this is what you want, it is imperative you have the knowledge, advice, and coaching you need to make decisions that are best for you.

Being able to choose your "process" depends on whether or spouse has already chosen the process for you. If your spouse has served you with divorce papers and chose an aggressive litigator as their attorney, you will be limited as to the choice you have. Being on the receiving end is difficult legally and emotionally. The spouse that is "leaning in" has a slight upper hand than the person who is "leaning out." What I mean by this is that the person who wants the divorce, the one "leaning in," is usually much further ahead of the person that is on the receiving end of the divorce, the one "leaning out." This could mean they have chosen the process without your input and have to come to terms with the divorce. Remember this concept during the divorce. It is very helpful to keep things in perspective if you are on either side.

The person who first makes the decision is usually further ahead mentally, emotionally, as well as in the legal process. Divorce is an extremely difficult decision to make. It takes a lot for a person to come to see me. Usually, the process of "uncoupling" is well underway, if not completed. Uncoupling is detachment and loss of connection to a spouse and a forging an independent life. It is when a spouse ceases to think of themselves as being part of a "couple." Because of this, it is usually too late for marriage counseling; however, whenever I see a client, I always ask them whether or not there is an opportunity to save their marriage, and I suggest counseling. If the answer is, "no," the next discussion I have with them is whether or not they want control of their divorce and to divorce with dignity. If you want to have control over the process, make your own decisions, and determine your own destiny, then an alternative process to litigation and court intervention may be a possibility for you. So now let's explore the ways to divorce.

There are four ways to divorce. They are as follows:

1.   Uncontested

This means that you and your spouse have few assets or have already discussed all of the items and issues regarding the breakup of your marriage. This would include areas such as the custody of your children, parenting access, sale of a marital residence, or who will live there, the payment of child or spousal support, and a distribution of all your assets and allocation of any debts. The attorney hired will draft an agreement and process all of the paperwork. The attorney will usually oversee and make certain recommendations as to what should or should not be in the agreement but will not counsel you nor will the attorney delve into, examine, or review finances regarding you or your spouse. They are taken at face value or based on submitted W-2 's, tax returns, or pay stubs.

2.   Mediation

Mediation is defined as an intervention in a dispute in order to resolve it. Parties mediate with a mediator. The mediator, while they may be an attorney and educated with regard to family law and divorce, does not act as an advocate for either one of the parties. Thus, a mediator's job is to facilitate discussions and navigate the conversation and discussion so that an agreement incorporating and including all the issues of divorce can be reached. A mediator can request information, such as financials from both parties. However, the mediator reviews and extrapolates the information from the financial documents that they require the parties to bring in; he or she does not analyze them, comment on them, or give advice as to what the other spouse should or should not do with the financial information.

If you and your spouse are knowledgeable about each other's finances, you filed joint tax returns, your spouse's income is reported, and your finances are not complicated, mediation might be a viable option for you. You and your spouse must be on a level playing field emotionally, financially, and intellectually for it to truly work. You can always take the final agreement or consult with an attorney outside of the mediation process after any session and then bring the comments and information or questions to the mediator in a session.

In mediation, the mediator should not speak with either party alone, and any emails should be copied to the other party. Any phone calls should be by conference call only. Any sessions must be made together. If for any reason the mediation process breaks down, and the mediator is an attorney, the attorney cannot represent either party. In addition, any information submitted or discussed in the process is confidential.

Remember, the lawyer-Mediator is not an advocate for either party. The Mediator is a facilitator and asks questions to glean

17

information needed. The Mediator should be well versed in divorce law so you have a well prepared, detailed, and legal final mediation agreement. The mediation agreement will be the binding terms of your divorce.

3. Collaborative divorce

Collaborative divorce is a form of alternative dispute resolution in which both parties hire collaboratively trained attorneys, and the attorneys and the parties make a pledge not to litigate and resort to court. It is also an interdisciplinary approach whereby the attorneys and the parties can decide whether or not they need additional professional team members, such as a financial advisor, a CPA, a divorce coach, a child specialist, all of whom are collaboratively trained as well. The process also gives clients the ability to be heard in a safe environment. Common goals are determined, and the team works toward their realization. Clients are heard in the collaborative process. Participants are listened to and not shut down as they are in the judicial process.

This approach and process is the most comprehensive and give parties the most tools for problem-solving and to fashion an agreement which can be creative, personal, and will meet you and your children's needs. Both parties must agree to proceed with integrity and transparency. If either you or your spouse is not willing to participate in the process, give whatever documents and information are needed, and work with their spouse—this, unfortunately, is not a process that will work for you. If there is domestic violence or an imbalance of power, this process is not an option.

The key ingredients of a collaborative divorce are integrity and transparency. I have been representing clients in collaborative divorce for a number of years, and I have found that most people can be part of a collaborative process if they truly understand it, embrace it, and realize that out of all of the alternatives on how to divorce it gives each spouse the most options, control, and the most attention and care.

4.   Contested

Contested cases/litigation are when a divorce is begun with commencing a lawsuit with the service of a summons. The attorneys proceed to "litigate," often placing the case on the calendar, and it is then on what's called a "litigation track." Once the case is before a judge, there are deadlines and certain rules and regulations with regard to producing documents which have to be submitted, appraisals, ordered, along with necessary financial information. Appraisals are ordered for any property owned by the parties, businesses need to be evaluated, and the pensions and retirement assets are evaluated as well. The parties must submit copious financial information, including bank accounts, credit cards, bank statements, copies of deeds, copies of any business records, tax returns, corporate records, etc. Of course, the extent of the discovery, i.e. financial requests, depends on the assets and liabilities and length of the marriage. In this process, there may be depositions of the parties, which is a sworn testimony under oath, and the attorneys ask questions of you and your spouse in the presence of a court reporter. Many judges require depositions be held prior to a trial being ordered.

One of the biggest and most important reasons to stay out of court is that there is no creativity in the law. We are stuck with statutes and civil procedures. Judges who do not know you or your history are determining your fate and that of your children. They get to spend your money, divide your money, and determine what money there is. Every judge is a person, and they have a history and a certain personality. They have their own particular worldview and agenda. While they try to be impartial, they are influenced by their experience, history, temperament, and "burn out." You do not know nor can you control who hears your case. Judges are human and thus not infallible. You definitely roll the dice when dealing with a judge.

If you have children, stay clear of the courthouse if at all possible. You will embroil your children in the process. They will be robbed of their childhood. Instead of playing, being with their friends, and participating in school activities, sports and activities, they will be going to "their" attorney's office as well as seeing a psychiatrist or psychologist if a custody evaluation is ordered by the judge. In certain jurisdictions a lawyer will be assigned to your children, and, if your children have different opinions, and positions they may need separate attorneys. You are stuck with the bill for their lawyers as well as that of your own attorney. If there is a custody trial, your children will have to be interviewed by the judge. This is called an "in-camera." Again, this is subject to the laws in your state. This is not an experience or a memory you will want to be responsible for giving your children.

22

Instead, be creative if you can. Make use of resources such as family therapists, a parent coordinator, a mediator. Talk to your attorney about avoiding court and request four-way conferences (face to face meeting in an attorney's office) with you and your spouse and both attorneys. Of course, collaborative divorce affords this and this is the procedure it follows. However, if you are not in a collaborative divorce, you can still use some of the tools of collaborative divorce, such as four-way conferences and use of other resources.

At a four-way conference, you and your spouse and both attorneys can have a discussion and air out concerns, hear different proposals, and truly delve into the issues. You will be able to assess if any of the proposals are truly well thought out possibilities, or if they are only a pipedream or wish list that is unrealistic. You can determine that at the four-way. Problem solve and use all the energy, knowledge, and talent in the room in the direction of what is best for your children. What will work and what will allow your child or children to have both parents in their lives? What choices will not financially devastate or bankrupt your family? Remember, your children are not divorcing. You and your spouse are divorcing each other, not your children.

FINDING THE RIGHT ATTORNEY: CHEMISTRY IS IMPORTANT

In the process of choosing an attorney, one must be wary. It is always helpful when an attorney is referred from a former client. In addition, it is best to meet with the attorney and see whether or not you have a chemistry and can communicate properly before hiring him or her. Questions to ask yourself are

1.   Is the attorney being honest with you as to what he or she can do for you?

2. Does he or she quote and explain the law and procedure?

3. Is he or she managing your expectations?

4. Is the attorney telling you what you can expect?

5. What is their experience?

6. Do they specialize in Family Law?

7. What kind of support staff do they have? Will they be able to serve you adequately?

8. Are you being heard and listened to by your attorney?

During the consultation and in your interactions with the attorney, assess whether or not they are listening to you. Are they making eye contact? Are they listening to what it is concerning you? Are they constantly interrupting you? Are they addressing what your fears are? Are they respectful of how you want to handle the divorce? Are they giving you options? Are they keeping you informed by giving you copies of all court documents, correspondence, and emails?

It does not serve you well to have someone who tells you what you want to hear in order for them to receive a retainer and then not be able to deliver on their promises. If you fall into this trap, you will have just wasted a lot of time, energy, and money let alone the emotional cost, devastation, and disappointment you will experience.

While an attorney's job is to advocate for a client, they must also consider what their client's wishes are. Remember, it is your life. Yes, you need to be educated by your attorney, and your attorney needs to advise you of what you are entitled to as well as what it will take to obtain what you are entitled to. A good divorce attorney tries to find out what is most important to you, then he or she should negotiate and strategize based on that understanding, and always consider your input within the bounds of the law. An attorney must always advise you of any settlement proposals or documents submitted by the other attorney. Attorneys who hold back for "your own good" do you no good and are unethical. It is your divorce and your life.

Many a divorce client has suffered as a result of an attorney not having the proper staff to be able to attend to the client. They must be able to draft correspondence, motions, pleadings, and review all of the financials and discovery for yourself as well as your spouse. In addition, it is important that your attorney be available to you and be able to communicate with you. Emails, as well as phone calls, should be answered in a reasonable amount of time. You should also have access to the office and staff, so you can be supported and your questions can be answered during this very trying time. If your attorney is unavailable, having an associate or paralegal address your concerns is invaluable.

When you are in the process, whatever form it may take, you must work with your attorney. Whatever documents must be filled out, whatever information he or she asks you get, whatever appointments are necessary to be made, bringing in necessary documents, or emailing information must be a top priority. Your attorney will only be as good as the information you supply them with and the efforts that you make. It is a relationship, and, as all relationships go, if you have the right attorney, the more you put into the relationship, the better it will be. An attorney can't go through the divorce for you. It is not our divorce. We go through the divorce *with* you, and having your information and cooperation is extremely important. If your attorney gives you a list of things to do, do them. For example, if you need to schedule a real estate appraisal or meet with an accountant, real estate or mortgage broker, make sure that you do this on a timely basis. and report back to your attorney.

As mentioned previously, divorce is expensive, so make sure you have the resources to pay your attorney. You want the best from your attorney and their staff. This is a reciprocal relationship. They serve you, and you pay for those services. Most attorneys also have a large overhead and support staff that they need to ensure their clients' success. An attorney cannot and should not finance your litigation. An attorney will likely not continue on a case if they are not being paid or have an expectation and guarantee to receive payment in the future as agreed to by you.

Your attorney must advise you whether or not it is feasible to proceed on a specific issue or claim that you want to put forth. While the attorney has the absolute right to decide the legal action to take, the client must listen to the advice of their attorney on the law, ethics, and legal procedure and cooperate with them fully. You must also be honest with your attorney and disclose all your assets, liabilities, and any issues that will come up. The worst thing for an attorney is to be caught off guard. Your attorney needs to know the worst about you. You must be able to trust them and feel you can confide in them. The more they know and understand, the better able they will be to fight and advocate for you. Having this relationship will help you survive and thrive.

The divorce and the process you choose will impact your children; your desire and need to protect your children is paramount. This is usually my client's greatest concern, and it should be. Children, especially children under the age of eighteen, are affected primarily by what they are exposed to during your divorce and how it is presented and dealt with. What they see and hear will greatly affect them and you in the future. The more acrimonious the divorce, the worse it is for the children. Based on findings and psychological studies of the importance for children to have a relationship with both parties, the courts base their decisions on custody on the premise that a child has a right to have a relationship with both mother and father. In addition, the courts in most jurisdictions also are under the assumption that parents should be making decisions together with regard to their children's health, education, and welfare. Unless there is domestic violence, mental illness, or an active addiction, a long distance, or a job or career which limits time and access, the courts will strive for as much of equal parenting as possible based on the parents' schedule and availability for the children. The issues such as domestic violence, mental illness, addiction, alcohol problems, and an inability to communicate will often allow the courts to fashion something other than a joint custody agreement. Unfortunately, it is also true that the courts fail to uncover or acknowledge when these negative issues are present! Abusers get joint custody all too often, and an experienced litigator should be sought if there is abuse, addiction, or domestic violence.

Unfortunately, many abusive parents get custody of their kids, as judges are notorious for being blind to abuse. Even if you know there is abuse but can't prove it, that is a problem for you and your children. Justice can be deaf, dumb, and blind.

I strongly recommend anyone in the divorce process attend therapy and have their children enter therapy to deal with the issues, emotions, and changes that occur in divorce. It is also a must if you suspect any type of abuse or neglect. Every child wants their parents to stay together, and no child ever wants to be in a position to have to choose between either parent. Children often feel responsible for the breakup of their parents, and negative comments made by either parent against the other causes irreparable damage to the children's psyche. Children pick up on tensions, anger, and the mistrust of their parents. Bringing a new partner into the mix during the divorce further confuses and muddies the waters. No matter what a child knows, he is part of both of you. Dad is Dad, and Mom is Mom, and you and your ex are his or her Mom and Dad. That will never change.

Therapists can give children the tools and support to deal with difficult parent and parental tensions.

For many years, I represented children, and it was heartbreaking having to ask them who it is that they wanted to live with. Of course, as previously discussed, if there is alcohol, drug addiction, or child abuse or neglect, you must bring this up to your attorney. These cases are handled differently, and the child, hopefully, would be protected from the parent who can't parent. However, the ultimate goal of the courts is to work toward the child having a relationship with the less than "ideal" parent. The hope is that issues preventing a parent to function properly will be addressed. The parent must get the help that they need so that they will be able to have a relationship with their child and be able to be a parent. The court does not punish but looks for continued improvements and a change for the future, even when this is unrealistic. Do not be under the assumption that only "good" parents see their children.

The ideal for children of divorce is that they have a solid relationship with both parents, and you can function as a family even if you are not physically together. By this, I mean attending functions together peacefully and making decisions together in a respectful way. Whenever you have to consider what to do, take a step back, take a deep breath and think what is best for my son or daughter. What would your child want? Constant strife, anger, and arguing are not what your child wants. Consider what is truly best for their psychological and emotional health. Stop and truly think and consider. Think long term, not short term. This way of thinking will lead to a better future for you and your children. You and they will not only survive but thrive.

I strongly suggest that anyone who is having issues with regard to communicating with their spouse or ex-spouse regarding the children seek the advice of a parent coordinator, a therapist, or a coach. Getting help, advice, and expert input will help you make the best decision. Many times, I have helped my clients write emails or discuss with them the best way to approach an open a discussion about deciding in regards to the children with their spouse. Parent coordination is a form of alternative dispute resolution. In parent coordination, spouses attend meetings with a parent coordinator to discuss communication and issues regarding the children. The primary object and focus of a parent coordinator are the children.

When I took my training as a parent coordinator, my instructor told me that she asks for a picture of the child whenever she begins a parent coordination intake. She then buys a frame, and every time the parents come in, she puts the framed picture of their children on her desk. Whenever parents begin to argue or not listen to what the parent coordinator recommends, putting themselves before their children, she points to the picture and tells them that this is whom she is looking out for and whom they should be looking out for as well. She keeps the picture after the parties end their sessions. I was touched by the box of frames and adorable pictures she kept and treasured.

A parent coordinator can help with regard to establishing proper email communication and protocol. They can help with limits, time for phone calls, or facetime with the children and each other, and establish guidelines and time frames with regard to emails, phone calls, and scheduling. They can assist with schedule changes, make time up and negotiating and planning vacation times.

When a major decision needs to be made, a parent coordinator can help with a dialogue and assist in gathering information that needs to be considered. The parent coordinator can also speak to the child to facilitate co-parenting. The goal is to help the parents co-parent. A parent coordinator can be an invaluable resource in helping to come to decisions and addressing any issues that erupt in parenting before it becomes unmanageable and leads to further litigation and more strained relations. This, of course, will further lead to more tension and emotional turmoil for both you and your children.

There is no-fault divorce in most of the U.S., and you cannot keep someone in a marriage that does not want to be there. Changes will be felt for the spouse that leans in as well as the spouse that leans out. This is reality. Protecting your children and securing your future should be the goal in any divorce. Most divorces can be settled. To negotiate and to be able to settle a case is much better than having a trial. Do not bypass or overlook this.

I tell all of my clients that going through a divorce is not going to be easy. Your finances together will now be separate and divided. There will be two households that are being supported by one income stream. Someone needs to move out. Expectations need to be managed, and the opportunity and necessity of having to make changes should be addressed. A house may need to be sold. A summer home or timeshare may need to be sold or transferred. One of the spouses may relocate to a different city or state. There are many changes that will be made, and, if you do not learn to bend like a tree in the wind, you will break. During these times of transformation, it's very important not to focus on your spouse, but to focus on you and the future. The "blame game" gets you nowhere. Spending all your time and energy trying to determine who is right or wrong is an exercise in futility.

Unfortunately, there will be times when there is no alternative but the litigate because of an untenable position that one spouse takes. Sometimes there is a lack of financial disclosure or hidden income and assets, which leads to a trial, and you can become embroiled in a tedious legal process. Again, your attorney would be best able to guide and advise you if you are in this type of a situation. If so, make sure that the attorney that you choose has the litigation experience, background, and knowledge to take on a difficult case such as this. There is an unbelievable amount of prep work for divorce trials, and trials are very expensive. You must have the financial resources to fund litigation. If you are a non-monied spouse and there are substantial income and assets, your spouse may be required to pay your attorney's legal fees. Again, speak with your attorney about your options and particular circumstances. Also, speak with your attorney about what evidence he or she has to prove at trial. What you know and what you can prove are two very different things. Again, consult with your attorney. Educate yourself and be realistic. The best way to know what to do is by having the best advice and support you can rely on.

Getting as much support as you can during this process is invaluable. As I have already mentioned, therapy for anyone going through a divorce is a must. It will help you with the process. It will help you be a better parent and support your children. Judges and court officials often look to see if a spouse is in therapy. It is encouraged and very well-received. Therapy will also help you discover why you married who you married and why it did not work out. If we do not see our mistakes and failures in our marriage, we are bound to repeat them. This is part of the learning process and a big part of the transformation, becoming whole, and flying free. Divorce is an opportunity to explore who you were, who you are now, how you got to where you are, and where you are going.

Using additional resources, such as a support group, a divorce coach, a vocational coach, a financial advisor to help you with a financial plan, a good accountant to give you tax advice and help file your taxes, as well as real estate brokers, mortgage brokers, etc., can also be of help. Of course, all of this depends upon your situation, and all are invaluable if you need help and can afford it. Your attorney should be helping you and guiding you to find the right professionals and talent to make the best decisions during your divorce and afterward.

In order to survive and thrive before, during, and after the divorce, you must participate in the process. The use of a coach who specializes in divorce can be invaluable to give you support, accountability, a sounding board, and to identify goals and the necessary steps to take to achieve them. Coaching is an innovative and creative process and is tailor-made for you. Consider it to support, educate and help your particular needs and circumstances. Consider a coach to help you transform from caterpillar to butterfly.

COURT APPEARANCES

Unfortunately, if you are in a litigation and require court intervention there are a few things to keep in mind, such as how to behave and appear at court.

At a court appearance do the following:

1. Make sure you are properly dressed.

2. Show deference and respect to the court and judge.

3. Do not talk out of turn when the judge is addressing you or addressing your attorney.

4. Use respectful body language while in court.

We have a judge in the area where I practice, and she constantly admonishes people who speak out of turn or to each other at the bench. She forcefully says in a loud voice, "This is not your living room." I understand what she means. Everyone has a turn to speak, and everything is done in order and a certain procedure must be followed. Very often, clients are so overcome with emotion that they want to speak out, or they become angry at something that the other attorney or their spouse says, which they think is untrue, and they want to shut him or her down, and so they call out. There is a time and a place for everything, and you cannot so talk out of turn or speak when your attorney is there unless your attorney tells you to. Practicing restraint is very important. What you say and how you behave can be used against you. You may think you are helping your case but it is quite the contrary.

The judge presides over the entire courtroom, and from their vantage point, they can see you, your spouse, and both attorneys. He or she can see when faces are being made, heads are nodding or shaking, or when you are not paying attention. Always turn your cell phone off when you enter the courtroom. Don't just turn off the ringer because playing or looking at your phone when you are before the judge will not earn you any points. There is a certain decorum to follow.

As I've said previously, no one knows what it's like going through a divorce until you're in a divorce. It is very important that you have the right information and guidance during these proceedings. *To be forewarned is to be forearmed.* This is the reason I wrote this book. To give you the knowledge and tools to

grow while in the divorce cocoon to break out and break free.

CHAPTER 2 - FINANCES

"For where your treasure is, there your heart will be also." – Luke 12:34

During and after a divorce, you need to make peace with money. If you never dealt with your finances now is the time to learn. You really have no choice. Think of it as an opportunity for change, abundance, and opportunity. Take the money challenge for the next thirty days. The money challenge is seeing what your money personality is, what you spend, why you spend it, and how you are paying for it. You will be amazed at what you will discover about money and yourself.

First, think about what your money personality is like. Are you a spender? Are you a saver? Are you oblivious to money? Are you very attached? Do you feel as if you never have enough? Are you fearful of money? Are you vigilant about paying bills or lax? Do you know your credit score? Once you develop your money personality, you can begin to confront why you feel as you do. It may be something to bring to your coach, lawyer, or counselor to give you an understanding of your strength and weaknesses, and then be able to work toward achieving balance.

The first key to dealing with money is to realize you can't print it. That may sound obvious, but many people live beyond their means and have mounting debt. Often financial strain and debt is a cause for marital strife and divorce. On the other hand, if you are fortunate enough to have an abundance of money, how will you use it in your new life?

The first place to start is to see where your money goes. Being aware of what you spend and on what is the first step. Keep a log either on the computer or in a notebook every time you spend money. Before purchasing something, ask yourself if it is something you need or want. If you are able to stop yourself before buying on impulse, stop and put it down. If you really need it, you can always come back, or, if you are too late and you are at the cash register, you can always return it. You will be surprised to see what you are spending money on and how those lattes, lunches, or clothes add up. Record and journal about why you made a purchase. Were you trying to feel better? Were you bored? Was it an expense incurred for lack of planning, such as going out for dinner because you had no plan for dinner?

You should run a credit check. You need to see what your score is and what debt you have. The main credit bureaus are Equifax, TransUnion, and Experian. Go online and request a report; it is very easy to do. To monitor your spending, you can find a number of free apps, such as dollar find, Bell Guard, and Good Budget. They help you track and even pay your bills. Many of these apps also link to your account, and some will give you your credit score.

How can this help you in the divorce? Well, let me tell you about Susan. Susan came into my office overwrought and overwhelmed. Her husband sued her for divorce. She was a stay at home mom and left all the finances up to her husband. She never wrote a check, used an ATM card, and had no idea of what savings or debt they had. I am happy to report we were able to uncover all the assets, retirement, and debt in the marriage. Susan and I worked together with a certified financial advisor. We were able to sell their expensive home and cleared all marital debt. Susan purchased a lovely condo in a community with a pool and activities in her children's school district. She learned how to live on a budget based on her income, had an excellent plan for retirement, and was going back to school to get her teaching degree. She is even banking online now. She is confident, hopeful, and treasures her new-found independence.

It's important to see a financial advisor to see review your assets, liabilities, and income once you know what you're spending and why. To help you get started in assessing and taking control of your assets and finances, I've attached a net worth statement we use in N.Y. It is an excellent tool to see where your money goes and what monies are needed to maintain your lifestyle. What I find invaluable about this form is how it details expenses we often overlook, such as vet expenses, haircuts, medical copays, etc.

After you take the money challenge and read the rest of this chapter, you will have a better understanding of your relationship with money and what your relationship needs in order for it to be healthy. The basics you need to know may seem dry, overwhelming, and difficult to comprehend. I will break it down as easily as I can and give only a brief introduction to help you know what you need to be aware of.

This outline will give you a general understanding of the financial vehicles you must be aware of during the divorce. They are as follows:

IRA or Roth IRA

An IRA or Roth IRA is an individual retirement account and investment tool individuals use to earmark money for retirement savings. It is an account which can be made up of cash, mutual funds, stocks, and has a defined value.

What's the same?

Contribution limits:

$5,500 (age 49 and under); $6,500 age 50 and older

Contribution deadline:

Tuesday, April 17, 2018 (for the 2017 tax year)

Minimum investments:

No minimum to open an IRA

Fees:

No setup or maintenance fees; no transaction fees for most mutual funds.

What's different?

	Roth IRA	**Traditional IRA**
Tax benefits	Tax-free growth and tax-free qualified withdrawals	Tax-deferred growth and tax-deductible contributions
Age requirements	Contribute at any age.	Contribute until you're 70½.
Income requirements	Your income affects how much you can contribute.	Your income does not affect how

		much you can contribute.
Withdrawal taxes	You won't pay taxes when you withdraw your contributions, and you won't pay federal taxes on your earnings as long as the five-year aging requirement has been met.	You will pay taxes when you withdraw your pre-tax contributions and when you withdraw any earnings.
Early-withdrawal penalties	If you make withdrawals before you're 59½, you might have to pay taxes on your earnings plus a 10% additional tax.	If you make withdrawals before you're 59 ½, you might have to pay a 10% penalty.

Required minimum distributions (RMDs)	RMDs do not apply during your lifetime.	RMDs must be taken starting in the year you turn 70½.

In a divorce, you may be entitled to a share of your spouse's IRA accumulated during the marriage. As part of your settlement, it can be rolled over to you, and you can set up your own account, or it can be taken (in a divorce) as a lump sum without penalties. However, you must report these monies as income on your tax return for the tax year of the distribution.

Stock

Stock is a general term used to describe the ownership certificate of any company. A "share" refers to the stock certificate of a particular company.

In your divorce, stocks may be held as part of an entire portfolio of a brokerage account, or they can be individually printed certificates in the possession of your spouse. Stocks have a value, and, if they were purchased during the marriage or your name is on the actual certificate or brokerage account, you are entitled to a share. Stocks can be split, so both spouses receive an equal share. If they are sold or if you receive the stocks in lieu of other assets, be wary because when you liquidate them you may have to pay a capital gains tax.

Stock Options

Stock options offer benefit in the form of an option given by a company to an employee to buy stock in the company at a discount or at a stated fixed price.

Your spouse may be entitled to a stock option as a benefit of his or her employment. There is a way of calculating the value of the option through an evaluation. Your attorney will advise you of that. Another option is to receive a share if and when your ex-spouse exercises the option. Your attorney will be able to determine the value and how best to get what you are entitled to.

Life Insurance

There are a number of different life insurance options. There is a term policy, which pays out on the death of the insured. What you need to be cognizant of is the length of the term. In divorce, life insurance is extremely important to guarantee future payments, such as for maintenance/alimony, child support, and future pension payments. A life insurance policy can be "whole" or "universal." This means there is a savings component to the policy called a "cash surrender value." You must know what type of policy you and your spouse have, as the cash surrender has a value to which you are entitled.

Again, be wary of whether you are paying out the cash surrender value because, if the monies are later removed, there may be a tax implication.

Annuity

An annuity is a sum of money paid to someone each year, typically for the rest of their life. It can also be a form of insurance or investment entitling the investor to a series of annual sums called "an annuity plan."

An annuity may be a part of your marital assets. Often annuities are retirement benefits for employees of certain unions or corporations. You may also have a private annuity. There are a number of ways to determine and split the marital share. It can be handled like an IRA, and, with a special court order called a Domestic Relations Order, or "DRO," your share can be rolled over to you. If there is a defined payout as in a private annuity, you can prepare an order that you will receive your share directly from the company at the time of payout. There is usually an age when the annuity matures, or, if it is a retirement vehicle, it is usually at age 59 ½ when it can be drawn down on.

Bonds

A bond is a fixed income investment in which an investor loans money to an entity (corporate or governmental) that borrows the funds for a defined period of time at a fixed interest rate. Bond values fluctuate, and their values depend on the type of bond. US savings bonds have a face value upon maturity. There are ways to calculate the value of a bond, and your attorney will be able to obtain that from an expert. Bonds are often split between spouses. Again, if you take bonds in exchange for something else, be wary of the tax impact it will have when it matures or you sell. Your spouse will not have to pay the tax if you alone receive the asset.

Pension

A Pension is a regular payment made during a person's retirement from an investment fund to which that person or their employer has contributed during their working life.

If you or your spouse have a pension, the marital share, that is the years the spouse worked during the marriage, is subject to division in your divorce. There are a number of ways pensions are handled. The most important thing to do if your spouse is not already in pay status is to get the pension evaluated. Pension appraisals are the regular course of business in divorce. You will be able to see what your monthly share will be upon your ex spouse's retirement. There is also a way to determine, actuarially, the present-day value of the pension. What this means in simplistic terms is that, based on your age, and amount of the pension they project the total amount you would receive from the pension over a lifetime can be calculated.

As the pension holder or as the spouse receiving their share of the pension holder's pension, there are a few things to consider:

1. Pensions income is taxable to the receiver (unless it is a disability pension)

2. If you keep your pension instead of receiving a share of another liquid asset, such as the marital home, the pension value should be tax impacted because the pension is not a "cash" asset as is a home or other liquid asset.

Another financial asset many people going through divorce have to consider and often have an attachment to is their home. They often trade pensions, cash accounts or other retirement vehicles for the "house." Oftentimes, they make this choice without having a pension or sufficient retirement savings of their own. This is why it is important to view the totality of your finances and possible ways of dividing assets with a certified financial planner and CPA. A

Domestic Relations Order ("DRO") will be necessary to divide a pension.

401k's, Deferred Compensation 403B's, and Profit sharing

These are deferred contribution plans that allow participants (in corporate, non- and for-profit or government-related jobs) to shelter money on a tax-deferred basis for retirement. The primary benefit of most tax-deferred compensation is the deferral of taxes to the date at which the employee actually receives the income. These retirement vehicles are handled the same way the IRA and annuity are handled. The marital share must be determined, and the nonemployee ex-spouse will receive their share after the submission of a court order called a DRO or Quadro. Said share is rolled over into a new IRA or other related retirement vehicles. If the plan rules allow (which invariably they do), this can be taken as a lump sum distributed, but it will be taxed as income.

It is imperative you and your attorney are fully familiar with ALL retirement and investment accounts of your spouse from current employers as well as past employers.

Mutual funds

A mutual fund is defined as an investment program funded by shareholders that trade in diversified holdings and is professionally managed. Mutual funds are investment vehicles. They can be held in one company, such as Vanguard or Fidelity, or they can be part of an entire portfolio in a brokerage account, such as Merrill Lynch, E-Trade, or Morgan Stanley. Mutual funds have value, and there is sometimes a fee if they are sold, depending on the type of fund purchased. The benefit of mutual funds is that they are diversified and often comprised of more than just stocks. Again, the key here is for you to have knowledge of the fund and to find out the value and what your share is. Can the fund be split? If traded off, what are the tax implications if you receive a particular fund?

Now you have a brief background of all the different aspects of the finances. You may need to delve into during and after your divorce. Given the possible financial complexities, I am sure you appreciate now, even more, the importance of meeting with a certified financial planner.

The financial advisor can prepare a plan based on a questionnaire, and tailor the plan to your goals and needs. A financial plan is best done after any life-changing event. Divorce is a life-changing event, so now is the time your attorney should be encouraging you to do this and referring you to professionals he or she has worked with in the past. If you are using a coach, a coach will encourage you and outline the steps to take. Your attorney and planner should be working hand in hand, making sure you have the security you need in developing a long-term plan. This is an investment in your new life.

I also recommend consulting a CPA about the changes in your tax filing, dependents, and to understand any tax ramifications of the proposed settlement terms. You will no longer be filing married. Especially with the new tax laws, it is important to understand the benefits and tax liabilities included in your financial agreement. Your attorney should be working with your CPA to afford the best scenario for you.

I usually send my client's completed net worth to their financial advisor. It outlines your expenses to maintain your lifestyle as well as all the assets discussed previously and your debt. It itemizes real estate owned including timeshares, vacation homes, stock options, and even trailers or Winnebagos. It is just another piece to complete the puzzle.

You have a choice: get a handle on your money, or not.

Harriet, unfortunately, was someone who did not get a handle on her finances. Harriet was given a plan after the divorce. She had alimony/maintenance of a sizeable amount for 10 years. She had a large cash settlement and retirement which she could receive at age 62. I encouraged her to go back to school and finish her degree in nursing. After the divorce, she did not go back to school, did not enlist a coach to support and keep her on track. She used her money for plastic surgery, for vacations with her new boyfriend Lance, (which she paid for), gave Lance money, bought new furniture, installed a pool, and bought a hot tub. Within five years, all her savings was gone, and she had broken up with Lance. She was lost and broke. She had tossed the budget, the plan, and "lost" my number and that of her financial planner. She had no willingness to use the tools and knowledge she was given. She went backwoods and got lost in the divorce cocoon. She could not find her way out.

Harriett finally called me. She asked about extending her alimony after her break-up and financial demise, and I told her that was not an option or the answer. She needed to reevaluate and get back on track. I suggested she hire a coach, meet with her financial advisor, and see a therapist to find out why she wasn't able to take care of herself after her divorce.

We met and I suggested she goes back to school, install the "Good Budget" app on her phone, and see her financial advisor to make an investment plan. Harriet now works as an aide. She is in nursing school, follows a budget, and she is building a future. Most importantly, her life is simple, and she is focusing her time and energy on discovering who she truly is.

After reading this chapter, completing the net worth form, and having a better understanding of retirement vehicles and assets, you will be better prepared for your divorce and afterwards. By implementing what I suggested in this chapter, you will now also know where your treasure lies. You will now have the power to create the life you want and be financially secure.

CHAPTER 3 – Physical Care

"The greatest wealth is health" - Virgil

SELF-CARE

Before, during, and after your divorce, you must practice self-care. During this period of transformation and change, you, as an emerging butterfly, need to receive nourishment, rest, and care. There are a number of aspects of being physically fit and healthy which are as follows.

1.   **Eat Right and Maintain a Healthy Weight**

Nutrition and balanced meals are important during this time. If you do not have regularly scheduled meals, your blood sugar will drop, and you will not be effective; you will have memory loss, be unable to think, and more prone to stress. This is something that you do not need during this process. There is enough stress. Also, even if you are alone, or it is only you and your children, it is important and will have great benefit for you to sit at a set table and have dinner every night. I usually suggest that people make up their meal plan for the week on Sundays, and, if it's necessary, to cook things in advance so that it's easier during the week to just warm up leftovers.

Sunday is the perfect day to do that. Sautéing chicken cutlets, grilling some fresh vegetables, baking a roast, making meat sauce, chicken or beef soup, are all things that can be used during the week. There are so many recipes and suggestions on the Internet. There is also Blue Apron and other companies that deliver the ingredients and recipes to you so that you have meal prep ready, and your menu chosen for you. Now is not the time to eat junk food, not eat at all, or bury your troubles in a quart of Ben and Jerry's Chunky Monkey. This will affect you not only physically but also emotionally. Choose fresh ingredients, vegetables, fruits, proteins, and healthy carbohydrates. Select minimally-processed organic foods. Drink water throughout the day.

2.   **Sleep**

Getting the proper amount of sleep is also necessary in order to have proper brain function as well as physical stamina. The divorce process is stressful, and thus your immune system is already compromised. Lack of sleep causes additional stress to the immune system. If you are not sleeping, you are also more prone to being stressed and being emotionally reactive. Some suggestions to make sure you have a proper sleep are as follows.

a.   Always try to maintain a specific sleep schedule going to bed at a certain time and   waking up at a certain time.

b.   Make sure your room is dark and comfortable, not too hot, not too cold.

c.   Reduce any noise that will disturb you. I actually have a sleep machine, which I turn it to the "white rain" setting, and it blocks out any traffic or noise that would disturb me. The sound is repetitive and has a hypnotic effect that helps me relax and fall asleep.

d. Do not use your phone or computer or have any difficult or long conversations prior to bedtime.

e. It's preferable to try to read a book rather than watch TV or look at Facebook or Instagram when you're trying to fall asleep.

f. An hour or so before bed, having a cup of chamomile tea or similar herbal tea can sometimes be very soothing and help you relax.

g. Lavender scented pillows or a lavender mist spray in a room also induces relaxation.

h. A warm bath or shower about an hour before going to bed is also helpful.

3.   **Exercise**

Exercise has been found to increase your immune system, reduce stress, lower blood pressure, lower cholesterol, and also reduce your risk of developing cancer. It reduces the risk of diabetes. It is also the key to longevity. Beginning some type of an exercise program during this process is very important. It can just be a 15–20-minute walk every day.

What appeals to you? I invite you to close your eyes for a minute and think about what you enjoyed doing when you were a child. How did you play? Did you enjoy running? Jump rope? Perhaps taking a dance class or a yoga class, karate, or tai chi will uplift you mentally and physically. These are all excellent ways of exercising, and learning something new will help increase your brain function and increase your mood. If you are interested in joining a gym, there are a number of activities and exercise classes that are offered that may be an option as well. There is also swimming, tennis, and gardening; any of these activities might help you move, get in touch with your body, and help you release some of the stress and feelings of anger, despair, and sadness that surface during this process. Feeling your heart pumping, your breath moving, and getting in touch with your body is extremely important and very fulfilling. When your heart begins pumping, your body releases endorphins which elevate your mood. Also, physical activity alleviates the anger and tension you feel and you help reduce emotional overeating. We are our bodies, and we need to care for them, especially during this process.

Other ways to release stress, such as going for a massage, a pedicure, manicure, having a spa day, taking a walk in nature, taking a walk along a beach, listening to the waves, walking in a forest, hiking, going to a farmer's market, or walking through a botanical garden, will help you elevate your mood and get you out of yourself. One of the biggest problems during the divorce process is that people become obsessed and so self-absorbed that they can't get out of their own way. Doing activities such as these will help you to get out of yourself and to connect to something bigger. Hug a tree, walk barefoot in the sand or grass, dance to loud music when no one is around. Adopt a cat or a dog. Caring for an animal can get you out of yourself. Taking a "rescue" animal into your home will not only give you pleasure, but also allow you to experience unconditional love. Having a pet reduces stress, and the joy of petting a purring cat, playing with a ball of yarn with a kitten, walking or "being walked" by a dog, and having a puppy cry at the door for you are experiences you will treasure. You need to remove yourself physically from the fight and drama and reconnect with your body & your soul. You are not your divorce.

While writing this I thought of my client, Dan. When Dan first came to see me, he was overweight, suffering from high blood pressure, and depressed. He was in a rut. He was a former football player, and he showed me his wedding picture; he was unrecognizable. He got up, jumped in the shower, and walked one block to the express bus. He sat at a desk all day and then took the bus home. He would eat dinner, watch TV, and eat a bowl of ice cream every night.

In the process of the divorce, I encouraged him to return to the gym, seek therapy, and join a football team. I also gave him the number of my hair stylist and masseuse. Within a few months, Dan had lost 25 pounds, changed his physique, and had a new hairstyle. He had more energy; his blood pressure was back to normal, and he had a zest for life. He had more energy for his children and was dating. When I saw him, I remarked, "Divorce agrees with you." He responded, "It definitely changed my life!" I said, "Sometimes it takes a divorce to break us out of our cocoon." This may be true for you, too.

CHAPTER 4 - EMOTIONAL CARE

"Wherefore, my beloved brethren let everyone be swift to hear,

slow to speak, and slow to anger." - James 1:19.

The word "emotion" is defined as an instinctive or intuitive feeling as distinguished from reasoning or knowledge, natural instinctive state of mind deriving from one's circumstances, mood, or relationship with others. During a divorce, your feelings are raw and volatile. In order to make the divorce process easier and to have a successful outcome having your emotions under wrap is crucial. You are on an emotional roller coaster, and the first way of managing your emotions is not to try to control them. You feel the feelings, but the feeling is not the reality. Feelings come and go. One day you will feel one way, the next day another way. In fact, it can change from minute-to-minute. You should not suppress or control emotion; however, you should not act out every emotion. Instead, we can experience them, acknowledge them, and choose how we act on or express them. Our emotions and feelings are all "guests in our house." The Sufi poet Rumi said it best in one of my favorite poems, "The Guest House."

The Guest House

This being human is a guest house.
Every morning a new arrival.

A joy, a depression, a meanness,
Some momentary awareness comes
As an unexpected visitor.

Welcome and entertain them all
Even if they are a crowd of sorrows,
Who violently sweep your house empty of its furniture.

Still, treat each guest honorably.
He may be clearing you out for some new delight.

The dark thought, the shame, the malice,
Meet them at the door laughing and invite them in.

Be grateful for whatever comes.

Because each has been sent

As a guide from beyond.

In order to be able to evaluate our emotions and be able to live with them, it is imperative that we allow ourselves space to feel this feeling and then have the breath and the pause to reflect on how you will react. This is a very hard lesson and one that it took me years to learn. I am still learning. Many of us grow up, and especially in our culture, we think that feelings are reality and that whatever we feel is the truth. This, however, is not the case.

Sure, during this divorce you will be disappointed, angry, afraid, anxious, and maybe even in despair. You will be depressed. This is normal. The support of a good therapist will help you uncover your emotions and discover and what triggers the source of these reactions. Often a catastrophic event such as a divorce will surface emotions that are long hidden and have been buried for years. How you react to your emotions will determine whether or not you will be able to process your emotions, and knowing how to react to them will determine whether or not you will be able to grow, be successful, and transformed in this process. Often times, clients over-react to another spouse's conduct or statement. These emotions must be handled in order for you to make rational choices on how to proceed and to make strong well thought out decisions.

This inability our of clients to exercise self-control is something that is extremely difficult for attorneys. Your attorney cannot serve you and advocate properly for you when your emotions are running the show. Being blinded by emotions will not only prevent you from doing what it is you need to do, but it will also prevent you from being able to hear and function. There is also a misconception that you must let out your emotions. This is a fallacy. In our culture, this line of thinking translates into yelling, throwing things, over-reacting, saying things that you do not mean, and, in the worst-case scenario, leads to violence. It is key to name the emotion, feel the emotion, let it penetrate deep within you and then let it go. What will derail you and allow your emotions to damage you and others is the use of alcohol and drugs, playing the blame game, secrets, and envy. Some ways of handling your emotions and creating the pause and space that is necessary in order for you to evaluate and process are as follows.

1.	When you're overcome with an emotion, take a deep breath. Breathe in, breathe out, and make a concerted effort not to speak or react. This will help you when you need to be in your soon to be ex's presence or during court proceedings.

What will derail you and make you emotional is alcohol, drugs, or other forms of addiction; using substances is not the way to handle emotions and will only exacerbate and damage your emotional health as well as your physical health. Self-medicating leads to self-destruction. It is also damaging in your divorce. Any issues regarding alcohol, drugs, gambling, or any other type of addiction are very detrimental in a case. It affects not only finances but, more importantly, will hurt your relationship with your children.

These types of behaviors can be used as evidence in your ability to co-parent. This is not something that you want.

2.   Attempt to remain in the present moment. When we are overcome by strong emotions, we tend to go the past and also project into the future. This is non-productive and dangerous. This will help you maintain calm, clarity, and be able to deal with what is important right here, right now.

Obsessive thinking can also be destructive. If you get stuck, and a thought or worry keeps replaying over and over in your mind, you want to scream, "STOP!" Remember that no thought is worth thinking about if it makes you panicked and anxious. Breathe deep and say this over and over. A frenetic, hysterical thought pattern will rob you of joy and peace and will prevent you from being about to function.

The blame game will also bring you down. When you're overcome with emotions, one often blames their spouse or someone else and deflects and projects their own anger and anxiety on them. It may sound cliché, but no one can make you feel a certain way. How you react to someone else's behavior and conduct will determine how you feel. The blame game is destructive and prevents you from moving forward and hearing what your attorney is saying.

3.   Secrets make us sick. If you have a deep seeded issue or hurt from your marriage or from your past, it is important to be free of that secret. To tell someone in a safe environment, such as a therapist, priest, minister, coach, or spiritual director that you can open up to. This is invaluable. It will release the energy that you are holding in that makes you unfocused and over-reactive.

4.   Envy. Comparing yourself to other people and listening to other people who have been divorced for some time can be very problematic. My favorite part of *Dante's Inferno* is his description of that of the place in hell where people who envy other people are described. They are depicted as having their eyes sewn

shut. Every time I look at someone else or compare myself with someone, I remember that disturbing vision, and I redirect my thoughts.

We cannot live someone else's life and everyone has a different story. We do not know someone else's story, and appearances are often deceiving. We each have different talents and gifts, and we were born and bred in a certain place at a certain time. To compare yourself to another is to do a terrible disservice to yourself and to the person with whom you are making a comparison. Many of my clients tell me how someone else was able to get sole custody in their divorce or have lifetime alimony or was able to relocate with their children or do "whatever." To make these comparisons is a recipe for disaster. Everyone's situation is different. No one situation is the same. Divorce deals with human beings, and human beings are unique and unpredictable. Do not drive yourself crazy comparing yourself with others. Especially do not compare your divorce with another. The information you are being given may very well be false. There are many factors and components of a divorce, and, when someone discusses their divorce, it is taken out of context. There are so many factors and the whole is the sum of its parts.

5. Writing your story. I often recommend to my clients that they write the story of their marriage and be very honest about the good times and the bad. I also suggest they start journaling. Writing your story and keeping a journal of your emotions is a safe place for you to identify, confront, and process them. It is also a way to look back on your role in what happened. Perhaps you were complicit in a certain behavior. Maybe you tried to avoid conflict or were afraid of change and overlooked a gambling issue, addiction, or infidelity. Were you comfortable not knowing your finances and, as a result, have no knowledge of your assets or liabilities and thus became totally dependent on your spouse? Maybe you were the

bread earner, and you were fearful of losing some of your assets and income, so you turned a blind eye.

This process of writing your story is also a very good way for your attorney to get a history of your marriage and also to see whether or not there are any legal ramifications of some of the history that you put forth. Keeping a journal through the process to detail your emotions, fears, concerns, and what good is happening currently in your life will help you to accept reality. It is a great way to be able to fortify yourself and persevere in the process. Divorce itself brings with it a myriad of emotions. You may feel abandoned, betrayed, and unworthy; you may blame yourself, blame others, be envious of others, feel angry, and as if your life meant nothing. You may be worried you will never again find someone else to share your life. You may feel that no one understands. Your particular emotions and divorce are unique. However, many other people have gone through divorce and were able to rebound, survive, and thrive.

Never lose hope. Realize that time will help the healing process, and putting these suggestions and behaviors in place will help you grow from this experience, and you will not be derailed by your feelings.

6.   Gratitude journal. Keeping a gratitude journal not only combats envy, it also brings joy and appreciation for what you have and for the simple things of life. So many good and joyous things happen in our lives, and we are asleep, and do not notice them. Just writing down three things you are grateful for each day will create a treasure of experiences and moments, which will give you an abiding joy. Just imagine a Starbucks coffee, the smell of chocolate chip cookies baking in an oven, a good night's sleep, a hug from your child, a hot bubble bath, a beautiful sunrise or sunset, the purr or meow of your cat, playing catch with your dog, and a good conversation with a friend. All this is happening, even while you are getting divorced. There is much to be grateful for. If you keep your gratitude journal a priority and stick with it, you will see how much

there is in your life to be grateful for. Research has found that people who practice gratitude are much more content and better able to manage stress and become less depressed. When you see what there is to be grateful for, it helps you stay grounded and remain in the present moment. The divorce cannot rob you of these precious moments or your joy

7.   Setting limits. It is important during this time of divorce that you know when to say "no." You only have so much time, energy, and resources. You must learn to take care of yourself first, and focus on your divorce. Sticking to certain behaviors and making sure that you are practicing self-care is most important during this time. It may be necessary to say "no" to certain social commitments or invitations as well as not agree to help with a certain volunteer project at school. You must conserve your time, energy, and money during this process. Just say "no."

8.   Over-scheduling. It is important not to set yourself up for failure. Do not put pressure on yourself by jamming too much activity into your schedule. Leave yourself enough time and space so that you can get done what it is that you need to get done. Every day, review and prepare something of an agenda or to-do list, detailing what you need to do, when, and how you are going to do it. If you are not being realistic with the amount of time it is going to take to do a certain activity, visit someone, or even getting to court or a meeting with your attorney at the right time, you must eliminate something. Nothing creates stress or sets you up for failure as much as trying to do too much in too short a time span. Playing the "beat the clock" game is no fun. At this time of your life, it is very important to focus on what you need to do for yourself, for the divorce, and for your children. Everything else can wait or can be done another day.

9.   Forgiveness. No doubt about it, divorce causes pain, and you have undoubtedly been very hurt by your spouse. Holding on to hurt and continuing to be angry and place blame on your spouse, even if they may deserve it, only hurts you. Forgiveness is a gift you give yourself. In order for you to co-parent, to be able to make the right choices in the divorce process, and to begin a new chapter in your life, you must forgive. Now don't think that forgiveness means liking. We do not have to like our spouse. We do not have to like their behaviors or choices. We do have to forgive and "love" them. The definition of love is willing the good of another. Forgiving someone will give you an inner peace. It will release so much stress and negative energy that you are holding and that is keeping you from being the best version of yourself. Resentment, anger, and refusing to forgive kills and blocks you from experiencing an abiding joy.

Forgiveness is a process. Don't think if you do it once, it's over. You have to forgive every day. It takes effort. Once enough time passes it becomes easier but it is ongoing. It's not a feeling. It is a "doing." All you have to do is say, "I forgive him," "I forgive her," "I forgive myself." Many divorced people feel as if they are responsible for the divorce or that they could have said or done something to have prevented the divorce from happening. They blame themselves, they blame their spouse, and they carry so much negative energy that affects them physically, emotionally, and spiritually. Cynthia Bourgeault wrote beautifully about the importance of forgiveness for "you":

"Everything that is tough & brittle shatters; everything that is cynical rots. The only way to endure is to forgive over and over, to give back that openness and possibility for new beginnings which is the very essence of love itself."

Practice the words, and say the words even if you don't mean them, and realize that, without forgiveness, you'll never grow and transform. You will not be free to live life to the fullest and be fully alive.

When I think of the damage lack of forgiveness can do, I think of Geraldine. Geraldine was an attractive woman in her late forties. She was well off; her husband was a successful doctor in N.Y.C. They had just had a party celebrating their 25th wedding anniversary. After the party, he asked for a divorce. He left her for a young nurse. To say she was devastated is an understatement. She began drinking heavily and was stuck on the fact that they celebrated their 25th together, so stuck that she could not move on. The divorce was difficult; she made unreasonable demands and had unreasonable expectations. Her ex-husband remarried and had a family.

Geraldine would not go into therapy, rehab, or hire a life coach. She lives in a world of fear and scarcity even though she has a generous settlement and long-term alimony. She crawls into a bottle to deaden the hurt and pain. She is in the cocoon and will never come out unless she forgives, allows herself to heal by practicing self-care, takes responsibly for life, and loves again. She needs to love herself first.

Now that you know about money, the legal process, how to care for yourself, and how to handle your emotions, you are thriving in that cocoon and ready to emerge as a butterfly. Now we will discuss what to do with the time you have and the beauty and wisdom of waiting.

CHAPTER 5 - TIME MANAGEMENT

"Teach us to number our days that we may gain a heart of wisdom." Psalm 90:12.

One of my favorite songs is Jim Croce's "Time in a Bottle." The idea of discovering what we want to do and running out of the time to do all that we desire hits home. It is tragic that he wrote this song and soon after was killed in a plane crash. Unfortunately, we all have a warped sense of time. We think that we can make time, we can stop time, and we can manage time. But really all we have is the present moment, and it is very important to focus on each day as it comes. Alan Jones, in the "Love's Journey," wrote, "The present is what the past is doing now."

During the divorce process, people become overwhelmed with what will happen, what is happening, wondering when the process is going to end, and how long it will take. This overwhelm is very detrimental to your psyche as well as the divorce. We can't control time or make time, but we can certainly choose to either waste time or make the best use of the time we have. Living in the present and having focus on the changes happening in your life will make the divorce easier and more fruitful.

HOW ARE YOU SPENDING YOUR TIME?

An exercise, I suggest that you do is you take a pad and jot down how you spend your days. It can be done on a daily basis or on an overall basis every week. You'll be surprised to see where your time goes. See your time as precious, you will want spend it growing through this process. You will use the time to explore the steps in this book and survive and thrive through your divorce, you will spend time building a new life and a new you.

We all say we don't have time to do something; however, you'll see if you're honest with yourself how much time is lost looking at Facebook, watching TV, or talking on the phone for hours.

Are you allowing yourself time to do what is important? Are you using your time to grow, to transform, are you allowing yourself time to just be? To heal? Especially during the divorce and after, you may find yourself with more time than you ever had before. Perhaps you have children, and now your spouse sees them on alternate weekends. For the first time, you are alone on a weekend or on a day during the week with no children. What will you do with that time?

KEEPING HOLY THE SABBATH

To have one day per week to do nothing but be with loved ones or engage in activity or hobby that you enjoy is so important for your mental health. That is why there is a Sabbath. It also enables you to maintain your energy and restore your balance so that you can continue to function as a mother, father, a child of God, employer, employee, daughter, son, teacher, lawyer, or doctor. To be able to spend time in any type of creative activity such as painting, knitting, dancing, playing an instrument is beneficial for your health and soul.

Think about what you did as a child. Close your eyes. Where are you? What intrigued you, what made you wonder and imagine? What filled you with awe and wonder? Relive these memories in order to carve out and recreate some "playtime" for yourself. What attracts you so you can go and play? In playing, you will be able to dream, to build a new life, and give you the hope and vision for your future.

In her book, "The Artist's Way," Julia Cameron talks about having an artist day. She counsels her struggling artists to do one activity a week alone that will spark the imagination. To do something childlike, innocent, and fun.

Do something totally different from your everyday life. What will fill you with wonder and amazement? Some suggestions may be going to a zoo, an aquarium, a park, riding a bike, take out a paddle boat, taking a walk along the beach, swimming in the ocean, attending an arts and crafts feast or flea market, attending baseball game or any other team sport you enjoy, playing in a baseball or softball game, riding a roller coaster. Anything that will get you totally out of your comfort zone and away from your concerns and cares and especially any thoughts about your divorce and everyday life will work. We need to have play in our lives and to truly enjoy our leisure time. Think of the word recreation. If you break it down, recreation is time to recreate.

So, what will you do with your artist day? And if you don't want to have any artist day, maybe you would like to attend a class or a lecture? Join a book club? Volunteer? Schedule a pedicure or massage? Part of having this time is also to unwind, unplug and enjoy solitude and time alone. One of my favorite things to do is soak in a hot bubble bath and listen to classical music. What will you do? You may be worried about what you will do with the time you have now that you are alone.

Constantly being busy and engaging in constant activity is destructive. Business is a way to handle and bury our emotion and avoid self-examination. Being constantly connected and accessible is a distraction and interruption from communion with ourselves. Turn off your phone. If you have children and you're concerned about an emergency, only look at those messages that may be from your children or an elderly parent. Vow not to look at the rest of your messages or emails. Program your phone with a special ring or sound if your children call.

Without time and space alone with yourself, you will never be able to discover who you truly are. You are unable to have clarity and clear thinking. A divorce affords the opportunity for self-discovery. You are ending one life and beginning another. You need to discover the child within. You need to see what makes you laugh, what makes you cry, and what makes you feel alive. I had one client who decided to become a Yoga instructor during her divorce. From the time that she began working with me to the end of her divorce, she became certified as a Yoga instructor and was beginning to teach classes. This all began because she was looking to reduce stress and took a beginner Yoga class when her husband first left her. Not only did she find something that helped her physically and spiritually, she found something that could also be her livelihood. This could be you.

Another one of my clients decided to take up ballroom dancing. I found this totally ironic because she did not have a partner. She told me that throughout her marriage she always wanted to dance, and her husband would never go. Her children knew how she felt and even bought her and her husband a gift certificate for Fred Astaire Studios on their anniversary. Unfortunately, it stayed in the envelope in a drawer for nearly two years. I encouraged her to take the gift certificate and to go ask them if they would honor it. The studio more than welcomed her, and they told her that many people come on their own and that the dance instructors help with the dances. She so enjoyed the one hour a week, she eventually was able to begin ballroom dancing. She actually met someone at a wedding. He was also a ballroom dancer and was looking for a partner in more ways than one. She not only met a dance partner but a life partner. There are so many possibilities and opportunities. Be open to them.

I was at an event recently, and they had "contra-dancing." It is a combination of square dancing and folk dancing. I was very reluctant at first to begin but I have to admit I never had so much fun in my life. I had such a good time. I found a place in Greenwich Village in New York City that has a contra-dancing group. They meet every month January through June. You never know what lies ahead, and what will be of interest to you. Life has so much to offer. You just need to be open to it. Use your time wisely, and cherish every moment that you have and celebrate your life.

WHEN YOU SHOULD "WASTE" TIME

My purpose with this chapter is for you to understand the need to capture the precious time that is leading you nowhere in the sense of helping you recover, heal, and be engaged in the divorce process. The question to ask once the divorce is over is, "What is fostering my growth and the mind, body, and soul connection?"

There is a "time to waste time." By that I mean not thinking of time as a space to be constantly filled with "productive" activity as defined by society, such as making money, working out, cleaning, organizing, taking classes, etc. Instead, I am referring to intimacy, friendship and relationships. This is what is known as "hospitality". The word is defined by Henri Nouwen as the creation of free space to allow people in our lives to experience us and for us to experience them. This is time to be open, attentive, inviting, and being together for the sake of being together, to not have a purpose or engaging in a competition, but just enjoying each other's company. Just being there for the other with acceptance, attention, and love. During this time of your life, having this support and experience is nurturing and healing. There is a reciprocity and mutuality, and time together is anything but wasted. Think of this especially when you are with your children.

Your relationships are changing. Your old habits of relating are over. Take the opportunity you have been given to explore a new way to live in the present moment, with a different understanding of time and how to spend it. Your divorce is and will take up much of your thought, time, and energy. Remember the analogy of the cocoon. There is a time for everything. This is your time.

CHAPTER 6 - SPIRIT

"God is spirit." - John 4:24

As you go through a divorce you need strength and support that is beyond this world. It is often not until we are knocked to our knees that we realize how much help we need, and we cannot do it alone. A divorce brings us face to face with our own weakness and our total lack of control over our own lives.

It was not until my second marriage failed that I was brought face-to-face with the fact that I was living a life devoid of soul and spirit. I was empty, and no matter how busy I was and no matter what I bought or where I went, there was a feeling of isolation and emptiness I could not fill. St Augustine said, "Our lives are restless till they rest in thee." My failed marriage also forced me to look at who I was. Why was I in one bad relationship after another? Was I living an authentic life? Was I wearing a mask or were my personas as lawyer, wife, and achiever taking over my life? Who was I? My marriage died, but I was resurrected through this heart-wrenching time of self-examination, soul searching, and refusal to remain unconscious. I discovered my false self and my true self.

If we live only from our ego, we are living on the surface according to the rules of a world. This way life does not recognize or embrace who we really are. To stay where we are and not grow, change, and mature is a loss. Divorce can propel you to take that next leap into the unknown. You can leave the false self and discover your true self. In order to become "conscious" and no longer asleep, you need to understand what it means to be conscious of the unconscious and how it makes up who you are. A divorce brings you face to face with these "hidden" aspects of your very self. Not taking the time and effort to understand and confront them will leave you lost, and you will continue to live in a haze.

Human consciousness is made up of several levels of awareness. They are listed in descending order.

1. The conscious level or self (with lower case "s") is that which is known, connected to the ego and sense of self including our thoughts, commentaries, feelings emotions, and body sensations

2. The Self (with a capital "S") is the totality of psyche/soul and is the Divine indwelling, which animates our existence. This is God within and an organizing principle of our psyche, which is the Spirit of God

3. The unconscious level, that which is unknown, includes ego, the persona, the collective unconscious, and the spiritual level of our being. It is made up of our deep-seated human needs for survival, control, and affection, as well as the attitudes and history acquired through myth, group over-identification, and cultural conditioning. It includes our woundedness, our traumas, and the residue of all the pleasurable experiences we have had in our lives. To put this

in perspective, think of this quote from Carl Jung: "We're about 10% conscious and 90% unconscious." The psyche/soul is described by Jung as a part of God. This means that God imprinted this in us, so we know He exists and is God.

The goal of the spiritual life is one of wholeness and peace, living from your true self. Carl Jung called this path "individuation," the process whereby the individual personality specific to a person differentiates from the conscious to the unconscious level. There is no better time to begin the path of individuation then now. Divorce means the termination of a marital union; you are now separate and are ready to begin a new way of life.

I want to share my own story of spiritual awakening. I walked into a Catholic Church near my law office, and I felt an overwhelming feeling of being home. I had not been in a Catholic Church for close to thirty years. This was after attending Al-anon and beginning to read and explore spirituality. I explored all the major religions and read extensively.

In Al-anon I discovered the twelve-step program calls on a higher power to help with addiction. Bill W., the founder, was a terminal alcoholic who had a vision of an angel in white coming into his hospital room when he had given up hope of ever recovering. His wife was considering committing him. After this experience with the help of a Jesuit priest he formulated the twelve-step program based on and greatly influenced by the spiritual exercises of St. Ignatius of Loyola.

Whatever your religious background, reconnecting with your higher power and tapping into that grace is crucial to maintain perspective, calm, and peace. There will be times you will think things cannot get any worse. To hold on to something greater than yourself can be a source of strength in this process of loss and change.

How to open yourself up to the spirit and find your true self and your own inner voice? There are a number of ways, which I will share with you in detail. Explore and experience them see what resonates and feel right for you. It will help you move from the divorce cocoon to transform into a butterfly.

PRAYER

"Call to me and I will answer you and tell you great and unsearchable things you do not know." - Jeremiah 33:3

Prayer is a conversation with God. It is an opportunity to speak about your anger, disappointments, hopes, worries, and dreams. It is spending time alone to tap into the recesses of your soul and listen. In order to hear, we must listen. In order to listen, we must hear. In any relationship, you will only grow closer if you spend time together and if you try to learn about the others. When we pray, we learn what is in our heart. There are many ways to pray. You need to know who you are and what you desire to fashion a new life during and after divorce.

Being in nature and exploring can be a prayer. Experiencing the outdoors is a way to get in touch with your God. Watching a sunrise or sunset, walking on the beach, star gazing, looking at a harvest moon, mountains, or an oak tree with orange and yellow autumn leaves can help you connect. Hug a tree. What draws you close to the source of all? Go! Take it all in. Just open the door and step outside.

Solitude, time alone, gives you time to hear and allow your inner voice to speak. Being quiet and without distractions lets you center yourself. It is a good time to gain perspective and connect with yourself and your higher power. Solitude and silence can be a freeing and liberating experience. Take a long walk. Pay attention to the movement of your body. Listen to your footsteps. Hear the rustling of the wind. Just be! What comes up for you? What are your hopes and dreams?

There are other ways to pray, which include vocal, meditative, and contemplative prayer. Vocal prayer is speaking to God and saying or reciting prayers, maybe from your childhood, a favorite poem, or meditation that resonates with you. It is petitioning God for help or enlightenment; you are trying through the prayer to make or trying to contact God. One of the forms of vocal prayer which is often very helpful for people that are trying to see their way clear is the use of the rosary.

ROSARY

The rosary combines vocal and meditative prayer. It is a repetitive prayer. While saying the rosary, you pray by following the rosary beads. I love choosing the rosary. I have a number of rosaries; some are merely plastic, others are more beautiful and precious in their look and design than some of my jewelry. It can be a work of art. The use of the beads gives you a rhythmic and comforting tactile way of praying. It is very real. There are a number of ways of praying the rosary. The main prayer is the Our Father on the larger single bead and the Hail Mary on the group of ten beads. There are five different mysteries. While saying the rosary, you can contemplate the mystery if you are so inclined. Also, each decade of the mysteries has a particular fruit of the mystery to pray for. For example, in saying the luminous mysteries, which is prayed on Thursdays and was instituted by Saint John Paul II the first luminous mystery is the baptism of Jesus by John the Baptist. The fruit of this mystery is the forgiveness of sin (separateness) and repentance. The second luminous mystery is the wedding in Canaan. The fruit of that mystery is the intercession and prayer to Mary to help you in the spiritual path and brings you closer to Jesus. The third luminous mystery is the proclamation of the Kingdom of God and the fruit of that mystery is to hear God's voice and to love, honor and serve him where and when he calls you. The fourth luminous mystery is the transfiguration of Jesus and the fruit of that mystery is piety, and illumination and the last luminous mystery is the Eucharist and the fruit of that mystery is to pray in thanksgiving.

I have found the rosary to be extremely comforting and helpful in my spiritual life. What is so remarkable about it is that it can be prayed anywhere: in the car, which I often do; while taking a walk on the beach; or while waiting in a doctor's office or in traffic. It has such a calming effect and helps you focus on God. You become involved in something other than what you're currently experiencing or obsessively thinking about. I often use it when I can't fall asleep. I will sometimes fall asleep with the rosary in my hand. I take comfort in something I once read: if we cannot finish the rosary our guardian angel will finish it for us. It is most helpful when stress, worry or anxiety overwhelms you. It is a spiritual antidote to the poison that kills the life within us.

RETREATS

During this time, you may want to explore going on a retreat. There are a number of retreat houses, and many offer programs for divorce, healing. and prayer. The retreat offers a safe haven for you to spend quiet time. It gives you time to breathe. There are different kinds of retreats. They can be directed, where there is a lecture or a specific program with a specific topic. There are retreats where you meet with a spiritual director once or twice a day, but you have time on your own. The director may give you spiritual read or scripture to reading and meditate on.

The directed divorce or healing retreats often have group sharing and support. They can be very helpful and healing. Hearing others' stories and ideas can give you a lifeline you may need.

During this time, you can feel isolated and misunderstood. Here you will be heard and find common ground. You will be embraced and connected to something other than yourself.

Silent retreats are also offered. I know this may sound daunting and the idea of being silent and alone may fill you with fear and anxiety. I do understand. I felt the same until I tried it. I remember how I was filled with trepidation and anxiety. How could I be alone with my own thoughts and feelings? No distractions. What I found is that the silent retreat gave me the opportunity and the "permission" to put away work, my phone, and inner chatter. I was allowed to be with myself in a way I never thought possible. The gift I received is that during meals I really tasted every bite of food I ate. When I went for a walk, I was cognizant of every step I took, the smell of the pine, the rustling of the leaves beneath my feet, the sound of the trees dancing in the wind. Without distraction, I could focus and experience every waking minute and every step I took. What a way of being.

Now I prefer silent retreats. It gives me such a sense of peace, and I am so much better able to put my life in perspective. I have found these silent retreats invaluable when I have to make a decision. I am away from distractions and influences. I have time to think and pray. This allows me to make the right decision.

SPIRITUAL READING

It is also very helpful during this time to begin some spiritual reading. Books about the spiritual journey, theology, or the biography of a holy person or spiritual seeker whom you admire, such as the saints or religious leader or great philosophers, are also very helpful. There is much to learn about the spiritual life. Reading and obtaining knowledge is a key to further deepening your growing relationship with God. It will help you understand your feelings by reading about others who had similar experiences. Your questions, doubts, and lack of understanding will be answered. You cannot love what you do not know and spiritual reading is a great means of obtaining a better appreciation and knowledge of the spirit. I have found such comfort and solace in spiritual reading, and I am sure you will too. There are many stories of great saints who suffered terrible tragedies and crises and found God in the process. They were able to live a better and different kind of life. One of fulfillment and peace this can be your story as well.

CENTERING PRAYER – THE PATH TO GOD

"Be still and know that I am God"

Centering prayer is a method of silent prayer that prepares us to receive the gift of

contemplative prayer, prayer in which we experience the presence of God within us and we rest in His presence. Centering Prayer is not meant to replace active forms of prayer, such as vocal prayer, like the rosary, or meditative prayer, like Lectio Divina. Lectio Divina is when one prays with the Scripture and places oneself in the scene or focuses on a word or phrase that touches them. Centering prayer emphasizes prayer as a personal relationship with God and as a movement beyond conversation with God to communion and encounter with the indwelling spirit. One rests in God and in the silence and privacy you experience the intimacy of relationship. It is a prayer of surrender and receptivity. This spiritual practice allows one to calm down interiorly. In the calm and quiet, a deep healing can take place. During this time deep healing is needed.

It is practiced by finding a quiet space to sit comfortably for twenty minutes to thirty minutes. One chooses a sacred word or phrase to repeat if thoughts are distracting and turning them away from God's presence. One can also use the breath, just breathing in and out. The breath or sacred word serves as a gentle reminder to us we are consenting to God's presence and movements within. It is as if we whisper, "God here I am."

The sacred word does not have meaning in itself as in vocal prayer but a reminder of consent and love. The sacred word can be the name of God such as "Abba," "Christ, "Lord," or words that connote the experience of God such as "love," "joy," "peace," or "mercy." The word is something one will be comfortable with and allow the transition to the contemplative state. It is best to choose a single word and to use the same word each time to create the space and experience to enter into the center of your being.

This was not an easy transition for me. I am very active and cerebral in my approach to prayer. I also have great difficulty remaining in the present. My thoughts seem to veer toward the future, and I have developed a habit of planning and always thinking about what is next. I also worry about making the most of my "precious" time. My mantra has been, "What am I accomplishing?

What have I done with the day? My ability to multi-task became a badge of honor. I began to realize I was always moving and that if God was speaking to me I would not hear Him because I was never in one place long enough.

Centering prayer is a spiritual discipline that has helped me listen and slow down. I am now better able to listen to others. I notice I remain calm when before I would become anxious and angry, often blowing up and lashing out. I still lose my temper but not as frequently, and I realize when I do. This is a discipline and practice, and, as the old saying goes, "Practice makes perfect." There are times I am very distracted; other times I feel consoled and peaceful. I realize that this is a relationship and like any relationship, it is ever changing and growing. I also know relationships take commitment and I am committed. I feel it has allowed me to make progress in the spiritual journey. I, like many in our society, wish to live more mindfully, which is being fully in the present moment, aware and attentive to what is going on externally as well as within me. Centering prayer has helped me in my spiritual journey to God, and it also has enabled me to live mindfully. I have been practicing centering prayer for over two years now. To be aware of God's presence and to remain in the present is no easy task. We often spend our time in either reliving the past by recalling past hurts and memories, or we are caught up in the future with planning and worrying about what may be. In reality, all we have is the present moment, and we often flitter it away. All God gives us is the present. He breathed life into us, and we continue to breathe with His very breath One breath at a time.

I recently attended a Centering Prayer Retreat. Father Bill Sheeran led the conference. He is now in his late seventies. He has been an advocate and proponent of centering prayer for years and has been involved in revitalizing the movement with Father Thomas Keating. He spoke of how it took him so long to realize that he was not living in the moment. He spoke of being dominated by his ego and his constant chatter that kept him immobilized and distracted. There is no true lasting joy or peace in such an existence.

There is an old Zen saying that if we are not in the present, we are in a constant ping-pong game of sorry-worry, sorry-worry. I truly understand this now. Father Sheeran told us that Father Keating describes our ego as a bridge that covers over the present moment. At one end is the past and at the other end is the future. The center is the present moment. To combat his tendency to not remain in the present, Father Sheeran developed a practice of paying attention to his breath. Whenever he catches himself leaving the present moment, he breathes in through his nose and says, "acceptance" and breathes out through his nose and says "surrender." It keeps him grounded and aware. If you think about remaining silent with God for twenty minutes twice daily, you may ask what will happen? I say, find out! Breathe in and breathe out, choose your sacred word, and enter into communion with God. Be in the present moment. Discover who you truly are.

Here are concise guidelines on how to pray and the benefits received.

1. Choose a sacred word as the symbol of your intention to consent to God's presence and action within.

2. Sitting comfortably and with eyes closed, settle briefly, and silently introduce the sacred word as the symbol of your consent to God's presence and action within.

3. When engaged with your thoughts, which include body sensations, feelings, images, and reflections, return ever-so-gently to the sacred word.

4. At the end of the prayer period, remain in silence with eyes closed for a couple of minutes.

The positive effects of the prayer are experienced in daily life and not necessarily during the prayer period itself. During this prayer, avoid analyzing the experience or having expectations. It is important not to judge the "success" of your prayer period. The only thing you can do wrong in this prayer is to get up and leave. You may find yourself getting in touch with feelings of pain, lust, or fear, or even remembering feelings or events you forgot about long ago.

* Enhances our ability to "Let Go, and Let God"

* Develops a nonjudgmental attitude of ourselves and others

* We grow in self-knowledge, which at times may be painful

* Emerging capacity to listen and serve others

* Nurtures our ability to live in the present moment and just for today

* You will experience deep healing and wholeness

123

During the divorce you lose a part of yourself. You need to reconnect with yourself and others, you need to become whole. You need spiritual healing, healing for your soul and your broken heart.

WELCOME PRAYER

The welcome prayer is a prayer on the go. It is an excellent means to create the space you need to not to react inappropriately to a feeling or situation you find yourself in. The welcoming prayer can transform your attitude about what is happening right here right now. We have basic survival needs the need for security and survival, the need for affection and esteem, the need for power and control. They are instinctual, and we are born with them. They are certainly activated during a divorce. They are basic needs, but, as we get older, we complicate these needs, and rather than them being to ensure we have food or bond with our mother during infancy, they become distorted and can translate into manipulating and rationalizing behaviors. A good example is becoming irate at a person cutting you off in traffic. Here the need to control overtakes us. The welcoming prayer is a way to make peace with these biological needs and keep them in perspective, so they do not rule our lives.

What do you do when your anger, resentment, or fear overcomes you and gets the better of you? Try these steps. The first step is to become aware of your body. When an emotion rises up in you, scan your body. What sensations are you feeling? Are you hot, feeling sad, cold, experiencing butterflies, or a lump in your throat? Sink into the feeling. Do not suppress it, hold it in, or deny it. Don't think about or try and explain it or name it. Just stay with it.

Then you can welcome it. You might recite, "Welcome, welcome, welcome." You are in the present moment and just accepting what is happening. After you make that connection, you can say, "Let go." You let the energy out as if deflating a balloon. It no longer has power over you. You now have the space to choose how you will react if at all. Doing this is similar to the slogan used in twelve-step programs: "Let Go and Let God."

One of the creators of the welcome prayer as a practice is Mary Mrozowski. She described the benefit of this practice in this way: "I am where I need to be, everything around me includes and hides the sacred." When someone challenged Mary about letting go and not resisting because she felt she was right, Mary simply asked her if she wanted to be right or have peace and freedom. This is a question we should all ask ourselves.

I challenge you the next time you are scheduled for a court appearance or a meeting at your attorney's office or have a confrontation with your spouse or practice the welcoming prayer. Ask yourself. "Do I want to be right? Or do I want to be free?" I guarantee the result will be beyond your expectations. Do it for you. I do.

EXAMEN

Another way to pray is to pray the examen. It is a daily self-reflection and self-assessment of your day. It is a way to "check in" with yourself. This has been a method of prayer and self- reflection since first instituted by St Ignatius of Loyola over five hundred years ago. It is a way to see God's presence in your life and where you were aligned with your spirit and where you fall short. I like to think of it as taking a helicopter ride over the events of your day. You may circle around one area and hover over because it holds significance for you. The question to ask is, "Where was God present?"

The way to begin is to find a space where you are comfortable and become aware of God's presence. I usually light a candle and dim the lights. I was recently watching an episode of "Broken" with Sean Bean, in which the main character is a priest. He always lit a candle when someone asked to speak to him or wanted to make a confession. He explained that he lights a candle to remind him and them that we are never alone. God is present with us. With this vision and once you are comfortable, allow yourself to feel God's presence, and ask for the Spirit to guide you.

Review the day with gratitude. Think of what you jotted down in your gratitude journal. See where you felt accompanied and what joy you found in the day no matter how small. Pay attention to your emotions. When did you feel challenged? Where was I kind? When was I not? How could I have done things differently? Then choose one aspect of the day, and ask for help and guidance. Maybe there was something or someone you need to forgive. Then resolve to do better tomorrow and make amends if necessary. Review your day tomorrow, and ask for a special blessing, affirmation, or help in the day ahead.

Another abbreviated way to pray the examen is to ask three questions:

1) Where have I suffered?

2) How have I caused someone else to suffer?

3) What have I done to alleviate someone else's suffering?

During a divorce, we can become very self- absorbed and unaware of how our behavior and words affect those around us, especially our children and loved ones. The examen is a way to reflect on our behavior, see what we have to be grateful for, and remember that the Spirit is with us and works in and through us. This is an exercise that will help you immensely in your growth and relationships with others during the divorce and after.

SCRIPTURE

Reading a passage from the Bible and meditating on it is also extremely helpful in the spiritual path. It is said that Saint Augustine had his conversion experience when he was desperate and praying. He asked God to show him what he needed to do. He then opened up the Bible, and there on the page it opened to was a line telling him that he needed to give up his wanton and hedonistic lifestyle. He needed to turn that wasted energy to discover his true self and God. He knew his heart would remain restless until it rested in God.

There are a number of ways that one can read scripture. One is to begin with any passage that may resonate with you that you have interest in. Proverbs, the book of Wisdom, Ecclesiastes and the gospels are a good place to start. If you read a passage, read it slowly and then close your eyes. Imagine yourself in the scene, and ask what is speaking to you, who is speaking to you? Imagine yourself as one of the characters in the story. What are you wearing? What time is it? What is the weather like? What do you smell? What message are you receiving? What inspiration? How does this relate to your own life and circumstance? What can you hold onto and pray over and help you in your struggles? What can you take away with you to help you on your journey?

A second way to pray with scripture is to read a line or passage three or four different times. The first time is to just read what is said logically. Then follow these steps:

Step One: Read the passage, encouraging everyone to **listen** with the "ear of their heart." What phrase, sentence, or word stands out to you?

Step Two: Read the passage again, and **reflect** on the word of God. Be aware of what touches you, a thought or reflection that is meaningful. Allow a minute or two of silence.

Step Three: Read the passage again, and **respond** spontaneously to the word of God. Be aware of any prayer that rises up within that expresses the experience. Allow a minute or two of silence.

Step Four: Read the passage a final time, and **rest** in the word, reflect, or pray, and allow the spirit to speak in the silence. Allow three or four minutes of silence. To extend the practice, after the resting, take the phrase, sentence, or word into your daily activity, and listen to it, reflect on it, pray over it, and rest in it as time allows during the day. Allow it to become part of you. What is Spirit telling you about what you need to do? What choices will you make? How will you honor and be aligned with the Spirit?

Another variation of lectio Divina is read a scripture passage and pick out a word or phrase that resonates with you, and hold on to that word or phrase, close your eyes, and say it over and over again, and ask the Spirit to enlighten you as to why this phrase is important to you. Why it has attracted you? What is the message it has for you?

These are just a few ways in which one can read the Bible and use it as a way of prayer, inspiration, and transformation. There are numerous Bible studies you can take. My advice is to start slowly. As you are becoming more comfortable, continue to delve fully into the passages. What is truly amazing is that you can read a passage or a line from the Bible, and then go back to it weeks, days, or months later, and you can have a totally different experience with that same passage. In order to understand our life experiences and human condition, the use of the Bible is a great aid. Use the Bible to understand, learn, encounter, and become intimate with the Spirit.

CHURCH COMMUNITY

Whatever your religious background, it is so important to be in community with others. Religious service on Sunday, a prayer service, prayer meeting, Bible study, a gathering of fellow worshipers, grounds your faith and prevents you from feeling isolated and alone. To pray in unison and to pray in solidarity shapes the spiritual life.

SYNCHRONICITY

Synchronicity is defined as the simultaneous occurrence of events that appear significantly related but have no discernible causal connection. This concept was introduced by Carl Jung, and he proffered the theory that nothing is a coincidence. As you begin to pray and become more aligned with the Spirit, you begin to notice how the Spirit works in and through you. Part of living a conscious life is being aware of the signs messages and coincidences that happen in our lives which we eventually see are not coincidences at all. Through the divorce process, watch for these coincidences and messages you receive. Sometimes they are from an unlikely source.

I am sure you can think back to times in your life when something happened and you later saw the connection. The key is to see listen, notice, and be aware. I will share a synchronistic even in my life. I have been meeting with my business coach to help me be more effective and efficient in my practice and in my personal life.

We have been working on what I need to do to have more time for my clients, for coaching, and spiritual direction. I often complain about how I wish I had the more time to work on certain projects I am interested in. He often uses the term, "create space." I had heard that phrase over many months. I had heard it over and over but I did not really "hear" it. Soon after I had to read a book for my spiritual direction training. In this book by Henri Nouwen, *Reaching out, the Three Movements of the Spiritual Life*, Nouwen uses the phrase "creating space." The premise is we need space (silence, solitude, prayer) to know ourselves, know God, and to grow in the spiritual life.

I had an Ah-hah moment, and it all came together as if a ton of bricks fell on top of me. It all became so clear and I knew what changes I need to make in my life to create space. It went from my head to my heart and soul. I am sure if you reflect you can recall these synchronistic moments. How many times were you upset by a change in plans only to find what occurred was even better? How many times were you thinking of someone or dreamt of someone, and they call or you run into them. By paying attention to these movements and being attuned to the messages sent by people we often least expect, we can move forward and live a life prompted by the Spirit. There are no coincidences. This is a sober truth to remember during your divorce. Pay attention to the messages and coincidences you see and experience during divorce. They may help you make the decisions and changes you need to be transformed.

Your discovery and relying on Spirit will give you strength, healing, and new life. You cannot survive, thrive, and become fully alive in the divorce process without the enlightenment, connection, and relationship with Spirit.

CHAPTER 7 - SPIRITUAL DIRECTION

"The spiritual director is concerned with the whole person, for the spiritual life is not just the life of the body or of the affections, or of the summit of the soul, it is the life of the whole person." -Thomas

Merton

If you have any desire to grow in your spiritual life, a spiritual director is invaluable. Spiritual direction is the practice of being with people, as they attempt to deepen their relationship with the divine or to learn or grow in their own personal spirituality. As a director, I listen and ask questions to assess the directee in his or her process of reflection and spiritual growth. Together we develop a deeper awareness of the spiritual aspect of being human. A spiritual director or "a holy listener" will help guide and direct you on your spiritual journey. If we want to improve our physical fitness, we hire a personal trainer. If we want to diet and change our eating patterns, we seek the help of a nutritionist. If we want to put our finances in order, we seek the knowledge and expertise of a financial advisor or accountant. If we want to understand our history, change our behaviors, and heal some of our psychic traumas, we seek the counsel of a therapist. If we want to grow in intimacy with God and get in touch with our spirit, we should seek the help of a spiritual director.

A spiritual director is a holy listener. It is someone who will meet with you on a periodic basis usually once every four to six weeks. They will listen, guide and support you in discovering your relationship to God, what your prayer life, is like and what God images you hold on to. Whatever your denomination, ideas, or history, a spiritual director will help you in your spiritual journey. I take my role as a spiritual director very seriously, and it is an honor and gift to be able to help in a soul's journey to the Holy.

A spiritual director seeks and asks for the assistance of the spirit when meeting with you. There are three persons in the room:

you, the Spirit, and the director. When doing spiritual direction, I keep an empty chair in the room, so my directee and I never lose sight of that. I would ask what your like prayer life is, what your relationship with God is like, what your image of God is, and I would discuss any trauma, attachments, or problems that you are encountering that affect your relationship with God.

We all need to tell our story. Everyone's story is different. Part of healing the wounds of divorce is to face your past, tell your story, and receive "attention." When you tell your story, the director holds it. I, as the spiritual director, am like a big and safe container to put all of who you are into. It is a safe haven.

A spiritual director is akin to a midwife helping you give birth to a stronger spirituality. During the times of divorce, it is especially important to have someone who can listen to you. I understand the pain that you are going through, and I know that grace and the help of a higher power can greatly support and heal you in the process. You cannot be nourished in the divorce cocoon and break out to transform into the butterfly alone. It is too difficult for us as human beings to do everything ourselves. We need spiritual help. We need grace. Grace and the spirit are akin to creative God energy to revitalize and nourish us. A spiritual director will not give you advice but will ask questions and direct you according to the movement of the spirit. A spiritual director is in sync with the spirit and in you. If necessary, I will point out something that you may not realize on your own. I may suggest certain spiritual readings or certain spiritual practices that may help you in your journey. You and I would explore different practices, ideas, suggestions, and see what may be a fit for you.

In my own experience with spiritual direction, it took me months of seeing my director before I was really and truly able to incorporate the holy and the sacred in my daily life. I tended to segregate it to a time in the morning, or at church, or when I attended a prayer service. Keeping the awareness and presence of the sacred with me throughout my day took time and many conversations with my director. With my director's patience and guidance, I finally had an "ah ha" moment.

I also needed months and months of healing, support, and attentiveness from my director to stop feeling as if I needed to do something to be pleasing to God and to deserve God's love and mercy. I also realized I never knew how to surrender and "just be."

Just like choosing an attorney—when you choose a spiritual director you must have a certain chemistry. However, when someone appears and you feel an inclination to ask them to be your director or if you receive a recommendation from someone, try and move with the spirit because this may be a message about whom you should be with. There may come a time after meeting with your director that you feel that the relationship has gone as far as it can and you need to leave. That is okay. As I said, a spiritual director is like a midwife and hopes to give birth to a spiritual awakening. Sometimes, once that is accomplished, it is time to move on to another director. Spiritual directors are trained to listen and should have knowledge of theology. It is also important that they have an understanding of the human psyche and life experiences, so they are able to relate and truly understand your story. They should be prayerful.

A spiritual director witnesses to your rebirth. You are experiencing a new reality; a new life and your spirit will be reborn. There is a period of patience, presence, and waiting. Then there is a transition where changes are slowly made, as you commit to a new way of being. The poet Rilke said it best: the key to the process is to "be still, patient and open." Think of the divorce cocoon.

The next stage is action. This means commitment to certain spiritual disciplines, spiritual readings, prayers and changes in behavior. This is an ongoing process. I want to offer you that guidance, support, and direction.

The spiritual life is a continual walking up the mountain. It never stops. We hike up. We have missteps, we fall, but we keep moving. Some periods, it will seem as if we are being carried up by a helicopter up to the summit. Other days, we will feel like we are always in the same spot and stuck. We are never stagnant. Every minute we are being healed and loved. Margaret Guenther, in her book, *Holy Listening*, said, "Our gracious God who can give new life in the building process to the most wounded and tired souls." Many wounds are deep, and they will remain on the surface and not healed through without his healing. Life and healing are spiritual issues.

When you are in direction, you allow the spirit and faith to color your entire life. It helps you experience and define the meaning of your life, where you were, and where you are going.

With my guidance in direction, you will discover it is not only up to you, and you cannot go it alone. The question asked is "What is God's invitation at this point in my life?" What lies ahead? Together we can explore and discover that.

A spiritual director is often called a soul friend. A friend who is there to help integrate your body, soul, and spirit into union so you are whole. Kenneth Lech, in his book, *Soul Friend*, states, "The air of spiritual direction is the achievement of the wholeness of life, an integrated personality, in which inner and outer man are united." It is not easy, and the crisis of divorce is a crisis of the soul. The divine physician will help remedy the crisis if you are open and receptive to the movement of your soul. Together, director and directee must learn to listen and be "obedient" to the promptings of the Spirit. The word "obedient" means to listen, hear, and it is an obedience of mutuality between director and directee. There is reciprocity, relationship, and mutual understanding and experience between us.

You are leaving a past behind to discover something new. It is a time to leave behind the false self and discover the true self. As a soul friend, I can help create a bridge to unite the two realities, so there is no separation or division. Entering into this relationship will allow you to be open to mystery and possibilities.

In my own spiritual direction experience, I found an abiding respect and exchange of ideas and desires. At my last session, I said, "I always feel so much better and clearer after I leave." To my surprise, he responded, "So do I."

Spiritual direction aims to help you transform your life. It is an exploration of your history, your present, and creates a free space for you to be yourself. It fosters peace and tranquility in the midst of your struggles. Through the use of imagination and wonder, new perspectives ideas and future aspirations may emerge. It allows play and new dreams. Karl Rahner said mystery, "is a state in which we are open to expect the unexpected and be able to play".

145

What is most intriguing and important about spiritual direction is how it unites all aspects of the whole person. If you want to embark on this journey of reef discovery, soulfulness, and wholeness say yes now.

DREAMS

Paying attention to your dreams is a key to open the door to your psyche and true self. Your dreams are a window to the soul. A dream can serve as a premonition or warning of a future event. It can point to something you are burying and not coming to terms with. During the trauma of divorce, old hurts and childhood secrets may be bubbling up and need to be healed. Healing cannot take place unless the wound is cleansed at the very root. Your dreams can be showing you a new direction to take.

Analyzing dreams can be done in spiritual direction as well as in therapy with a Jungian analyst. There are also dream workshops that work with a group that listens to your dreams and then helps interpret them by asking questions. It is another spiritual tool to help discover your true self.

Keep a pad by your bed, and, if you have a dream during the night and wake up, jot it down. Upon rising the morning, take a few moments while you are waiting for the coffee or tea to brew, then jot down images you remember. This is the place to start. You may observe patterns or recurring images or a particular theme in your dreams. This is a beginning. It is just another way to examine and be conscious of your life, sleeping or awake.

CHAPTER 8 - CONCLUSION

"What you are is God's gift to you. What you become is your gift to

God."

-Hans Urs Von Balthasar

The Butterfly Emerges

Where do we go from here? The answer is to leave the cocoon and become the butterfly. We must continue to evolve and grow or else we will not be fully alive and will die. We will just exist and remain unconscious if we do not continue on. This is not living. Your divorce gives you the opportunity to live.

There is much to do, and you must do it every day. How do you follow the roadmap given? How do you stay on track? What do you do when you feel there is no time? When do you become discouraged and lose your enthusiasm and zeal? You will need support. The answer is a coach. You need some accountability.

Someone to cheer you on to become the most unique beautiful butterfly you were meant to be.

I have always found if I do not have that accountability, I falter. I need someone to outline goals and listen to my dilemmas and the roadblocks I face. Someone to share in my doubts, anxieties, and fears, as well as my desires, ideas, and my struggles. Everyone is different. You may need support only for the divorce, for taking care of yourself physically, or a counselor for some deep-seated trauma or physiological issue. Perhaps you need help with the entire program. Help is here. If you follow the guidelines of this program, you will be a new you. You will not only be divorced, but the true you also will emerge. Divorce was the catalyst to get you here.

I want you to be able to transform your life. By the time you are at this place, you will, hopefully, have had a dignified divorce, have your finances in order, have a better understanding of your emotions, how to use your time, and, in the process, discover your relationship with God and the spirit.

The transformation process needs nourishment, commitment, encouragement, and support. Coaching and spiritual direction are ways to have the resources and fellowship you need to flourish. I am here for that support and be the bridge to your new life. I want to tell you about Camille. Camille met me at a talk I gave to social workers about divorce. She was having marital difficulties. She was stuck and her growth was stunted. She came and consulted me. We explored the different processes. She and her husband chose collaborative divorce. She and her husband chose to enter into a separation agreement. She so embraced the concept of collaboration that she trained and became a divorce coach. We became friends, and I began to coach her.

Since she met me, Camille has expanded her therapy practice, started a divorce support group, went on a pilgrimage to

Italy, returned to the Catholic Church, developed and active prayer practice, and has gone on her first silent retreat. In mid-life, she is calm and joyful, and has found her true self. She is transformed. Camille recently joked with me that she wonders what took her so long to make the changes she needed to make. Take a cue from Camille and begin now. Why wait? Don't you want to be fully alive?

I can be your coach too and keep you on track. Whatever aspect of your life, I can be there for you. I can help navigate the way with resources, support, and accountability. I can be your spiritual director and soul friend. Most importantly, I can be your container! A safe place for you to tell your story and pour out your heart and soul. I can receive you with openness, compassion, and love. You need a safe place. I can advise you, direct you, support you and help you.

Once you begin this path, you cannot go back. You will see things differently, feel differently, and realize you left the old you in your pre-divorced life. As you strengthen your body and mind, understand your emotions, and cooperate with God's grace, you will become the best version of yourself. St. Paul shared his struggles, "Be renewed in the spirit of your minds, and put on the new self.". (Ephesians 4:23-24).

Understand, you will not move on a continuous straight line. There will be many twists and turns, detours and missteps. Moving from what you know, your old way of life, to something new can feel as if we are being led to the desert left to die. What we need to cling to is that there is an oasis there if we keep moving and searching. You just dust yourself off and begin again, never losing sight of the finish line. Habits are behaviors we repeat over and over again. It takes time to develop new ones. With commitment, desire, and support, you can make it out of the cocoon and emerge as the butterfly. The butterfly will continue on the journey, it does not end until you take your last breath.

When you become discouraged, remember the famous words of Julia of Norwich, "and all shall be well; all shall be well". Indeed, all shall be well.

SUPREME COURT OF THE STATE OF NEW YORK
COUNTY OF

---X

                                                Plaintiff,

STATEMENT

OF NET WORTH

DATED:
        - against -

Index No.

Date Action Commenced:

                                          Defendant.

---X

Complete all items, marking "NONE", "INAPPLICABLE" and "UNKNOWN", if appropriate

STATE OF NEW YORK   )
)ss.:
COUNTY OF _____   )

_____, the Plaintiff/Defendant herein, being duly sworn, deposes and says that, **subject to the penalties of perjury**, the following is an accurate statement as of _____, __ , **20__** , of my net worth (assets of whatsoever kind and nature and wherever situated minus liabilities), **statement of income from all sources** and statement of assets transferred of whatsoever kind and nature and wherever situated and statement of expenses:

I. FAMILY DATA

(a)	Plaintiff's date of birth:	
(b)	Defendant's date of birth:	
(c)	Date married:	
(d)	Names and dates of birth of Child(ren) of the marriage:	
(e)	Minor child(ren) of prior marriage:	
(f)	Custody of child(ren) of prior marriage:	
(g)	Plaintiff's present address:	
	Defendant's present address:	
(h)	Occupation/Employer of Plaintiff:	
	Occupation/Employer of Defendant:	

II. **EXPENSES**: (**List your current expenses** on a monthly basis. If there has been any change in these expenses during the recent past please indicate). Items included under "other" should be listed separately with separate dollar amounts.)

(a)		**Housing: Monthly**	
	1.	Mortgage/Co-op Loan	
	2.	Home Equity Line of Credit/Second Mortgage	
	3.	Real Estate Taxes **(if not included in mortgage payment)**	
	4.	Homeowners/Renter's Insurance	
	5.	Homeowner's Association/Maintenance charges/Condominium Charges	
	6.	Rent	
	7.	Other	
		TOTAL: HOUSING	
(b)		**Utilities: Monthly**	
	1.	Fuel Oil/Gas	
	2.	Electric	
	3.	Telephone (land line)	

	4.	Mobile Phone	
	5.	Cable/Satellite TV	
	6.	Internet	
	7.	Alarm	
	8.	Water	
	9.	Other	
		TOTAL: UTILITIES	

(c)		**Food: Monthly**	
	1.	Groceries	
	2.	Dining Out/Take Out	
	3.	Other	
		TOTAL: FOOD	
(d)		**Clothing: Monthly**	
	1.	Yourself	
	2.	Child(ren)	
	3.	Dry Cleaning	
	4.	Other	
		TOTAL: CLOTHING	
(e)		**Insurance: Monthly**	
	1.	Life	
	2.	Fire, theft and liability and personal articles policy	
	3.	Automotive	
	4.	Umbrella Policy	
	5.	Medical Plan	
		5A. Medical Plan for yourself (Including name of carrier and name of insured)	

		5B. Medical Plan for children (Including name of carrier and name of insured)	
	6.	Dental Plan	
	7.	Optical Plan	
	8.	Disability	

	9.	Worker's Compensation	
	10.	Long Term Care Insurance	
	11.	Other	
		TOTAL: INSURANCE	
(f)		**Unreimbursed Medical: Monthly**	
	1.	Medical	
	2.	Dental	
	3.	Optical	
	4.	Pharmaceutical	
	5.	Surgical, Nursing, Hospital	
	6.	Psychotherapy	
	7.	Other	
		TOTAL: UNREIMBURSED MEDICAL	
(g)		**Household Maintenance: Monthly**	
	1.	Repairs/Maintenance	
	2.	Gardening/landscaping	
	3.	Sanitation/carting	
	4.	Snow Removal	
	5.	Extermination	

	6.	Other	
		TOTAL: HOUSEHOLD MAINTENANCE	
(h)		**Household Help: Monthly**	
	1.	Domestic (housekeeper, etc.)	
	2.	Nanny/Au Pair/Child Care	
	3.	Babysitter	
	4.	Other	
		TOTAL: HOUSEHOLD HELP	
(i)		**Automobile: Monthly** (List data for each car separately)	
		Year:_____ Make:_____ Personal:_____ Business:_____	
	1.	Lease or Loan Payments (**indicate lease term**)	
	2.	Gas and Oil	
	3.	Repairs	
	4.	Car Wash	
	5.	Parking and tolls	
	6.	Other	
		TOTAL: AUTOMOTIVE	

(j)		**Education Costs: Monthly**	
	1.	Nursery and Pre-school	
	2.	Primary and Secondary	
	3.	College	
	4.	Post-Graduate	
	5.	Religious Instruction	
	6.	School Transportation	
	7.	School Supplies/Books	
	8.	School Lunches	
	9.	Tutoring	
	10.	School Events	
	11.	Child(ren)'s extra-curricular and educational enrichment activities (Dance, Music, Sports, etc.)	
	12.	Other	
		TOTAL: EDUCATION	
(k)		**Recreational: Monthly**	
	1.	Vacations	
	2.	Movies, Theatre, Ballet, Etc.	
	3.	Music (Digital or Physical Media)	
	4.	Recreation Clubs and Memberships	

	5.	Activities for yourself	
	6.	Health Club	
	7.	Summer Camp	
	8.	Birthday party costs for your child(ren)	
	9.	Other	
		TOTAL: RECREATIONAL	
(l)		**Income Taxes: Monthly**	
	1.	Federal	
	2.	State	
	3.	City	
	4.	Social Security and Medicare	
	5.	Number of dependents claimed in prior tax year	
	6.	**List any refund received by you for prior tax year**	
		TOTAL: INCOME TAXES	
(m)		**Miscellaneous: Monthly**	
	1.	Beauty parlor/Barber/Spa	
	2.	Toiletries/Non-Prescription Drugs	

	3.	Books, magazines, newspapers	
	4.	Gifts to others	
	5.	Charitable contributions	
	6.	Religious organizations dues	
	7.	Union and organization dues	
	8.	Commutation expenses	
	9.	Veterinarian/pet expenses	

	10.	Child support payments (for Child(ren) of a prior marriage or relationship pursuant to court order or agreement)	
	11.	Alimony and maintenance payments (prior marriage pursuant to court order or agreement)	
	12.	Loan payments	
	13.	Unreimbursed business expenses	
	14.	Safe Deposit Box rental fee	
		TOTAL: MISCELLANEOUS	
(n)		**Other: Monthly**	
	1.		
	2.		
	3.		
		TOTAL: OTHER	
		TOTAL: MONTHLY EXPENSES	

III.		**GROSS INCOME INFORMATION:**	
	(a)	Gross (total) income - as should have been or should be reported in the most recent Federal income tax return. (State whether your income has changed during the year preceding date of this affidavit. If so, please explain.) **Attach most recent W-2, 1099s, K1s and income tax returns.** **List any amount deducted from gross income for retirement benefits or tax deferred savings.**	
	(b)	To the extent not already included in gross income in (a) above:	

		1. Investment income, including interest and
		     dividend income, reduced by sums expended
		     in connection with such investment	

		2. Worker's compensation **(indicate percentage of amount due to lost wages)**	
		3. Disability benefits **(indicate percentage of amount due to lost wages)**	
		4. Unemployment insurance benefits	

		5. Social Security benefits	
		6. Supplemental Security Income	
		7. Public assistance	
		8. Food stamps	
		9. Veterans benefits	
		10. Pensions and retirement benefits	
		11. Fellowships and stipends	
		12. Annuity payments	
	(c)	If any child or other member of your household is employed, set forth name and that person's annual income:	
	(d)	List any maintenance and/or child support you are receiving pursuant to court order or agreement	
	(e)	Other:	

IV. <u>ASSETS</u> *(If any asset is held jointly with spouse or another, so state, and set forth   your respective shares. Attach additional sheets, if needed)*

A.	1.	Cash Accounts:	
		Cash	
		1.1 a. Location	
		b. Source of Funds	
		c. Amount as of date of commencement	
		d. Current amount	
		TOTAL: CASH	
	2.	Checking Accounts:	
		2.1 a. Financial Institution	
		b. Account Number	
		c. Title holder	
		d. Date opened	
		e. Source of Funds	
		f. Balance as of date of commencement	
		g. Current balance	

		2.2 a. Financial Institution	
		b. Account Number	
		c. Title holder	
		d. Date opened	
		e. Source of Funds	
		f. Balance as of date of commencement	
		g. Current balance	
		TOTAL: Checking Accounts	

	3.	Savings Account (including individual, joint, totten trust, certificates of deposit, treasury notes)	
		3.1 a. Financial Institution	
		b. Account Number	
		c. Title holder	
		d. Type of account	
		e. Date opened	
		f. Source of Funds	
		g. Balance as of date of commencement	
		h. Current balance	
		3.2 a. Financial Institution	
		b. Account Number	
		c. Title holder	
		d. Type of account	
		e. Date opened	
		f. Source of Funds	
		g. Balance as of date of commencement	
		h. Current balance	

		TOTAL: Savings Accounts	
		TOTAL: Accounts	$
B.	4.	Real Estate (Including real property, leaseholds, life estates, etc. at market value – do not deduct any mortgage)	
		4.1 a. Description	
		b. Title owner	
		c. Date of acquisition	
		d. Original price	

		e. Source of funds to acquire	
		f. Amount of mortgage or lien unpaid	
		g. Estimate current fair market value	
		4.2 a. Description	
		b. Title owner	
		c. Date of acquisition	
		d. Original price	
		e. Source of funds to acquire	
		f. Amount of mortgage or lien unpaid	
		g. Estimate current fair market value	
		TOTAL: Real Estate	
C.	5.	Retirement Accounts (e.g. IRAs, 401(k)s, 403(b)s, pension, profit sharing plans, deferred compensation plans, etc.)	
		5.1 a. Description	
		b. Location of assets	
		c. Title owner	

		d. Date of acquisition	
		e. Source of funds	
		f. Amount of unpaid liens	
		g. Value as of date of commencement	
		h. Current value	
		5.2 a. Description	
		b. Location of assets	
		c. Title owner	
		d. Date of acquisition	
		e. Source of funds	

		f. Amount of unpaid liens	
		g. Value as of date of commencement	
		h. Current value	
		TOTAL: Retirement Accounts	
D.	6.	Vehicles (Auto, Boat, Truck, Plane, Camper, Motorcycles, etc.)	
		6.1 a. Description	
		b. Title owner	
		c. Date of acquisition	
		d. Original price	
		e. Source of funds to acquire	
		f. Amount of lien unpaid	
		g. Current fair market value	
		h. Value as of date of commencement	
		6.2 a. Description	
		b. Title owner	
		c. Date of acquisition	
		d. Original price	
		e. Source of funds to acquire	
		f. Amount of lien unpaid	

		g. Current fair market value	
		h. Value as of date of commencement	
		TOTAL: Value of Vehicles	$
E.	7.	Jewelry, art, antiques, household furnishings, precious objects, gold and precious metals (only if valued at more than $500)	
		7.1 a. Description	
		b. Title owner	

		c. Location	
		d. Original price or value	
		e. Source of funds to acquire	
		f. Amount of lien unpaid	
		g. Value as of date of commencement	
		h. Estimate Current Value	
		7.2 a. Description	
		b. Title Owner	
		c. Location	
		d. Original price or value	
		e. Source of funds to acquire	
		f. Amount of lien unpaid	
		g. Value as of date of commencement	
		h. Estimate Current Value	
		TOTAL Value of Jewelry, Art, Antiques, etc.	$

		IF YOU HAVE NO OTHER ASSETS OR BUSINESS INTERESTS, GO TO THE LIABILITIES SECTION ON PAGE 17	
F.	8.	Interest in any Business	
		8.1 a. Name and Address of Business	
		b. Type of Business (corporate, partnership, sole proprietorship or other)	
		c. Your percentage of interest	
		d. Date of acquisition	
		e. Original price or value	

		f. Source of funds to acquire	
		g. Net worth of business and date of such valuation	
		h. Other relevant information	
		TOTAL: Value of Business Interests	
G.	9.	Cash Surrender Value of Life Insurance	
		9.1 a. Insurer's name and address	
		b. Name of insured	
		c. Policy number	
		d. Face amount of policy	
		e. Policy owner	
		f. Date of acquisition	
		g. Source of funds	
		h. Cash surrender value as of date of commencement	
		i. Current cash surrender value	
		9.2 a. Insurer's name and address	
		b. Name of insured	
		c. Policy number	
		d. Face amount of policy	

		e. Policy owner	
		f. Date of acquisition	
		g. Source of funds	
		h. Cash surrender value as of date of commencement	
		i. Current cash surrender value	
		Total: Cash Surrender Value of Life Insurance	

H.	10.	Investment Accounts/Securities/Stock Options/Commodities/Broker Margin Accounts	
		10.1 a. Description	
		b. Title holder	
		c. Location	
		d. Date of acquisition	
		e. Source of funds	
		f. Value as of date of commencement	
		g. Current value	
		10.2 a. Description	
		b. Title holder	
		c. Location	
		d. Date of acquisition	
		e. Source of funds	
		f. Value as of date of commencement	
		g. Current Value	
		TOTAL: Investment Accounts/Securities/Stock Options/Commodities/Broker Margin Accounts	

		TOTAL: Value of Securities	$
I.	11.	Loans to Others and Accounts Receivable	
		11.1 a. Debtor's Name and Address	
		b. Original amount of loan or debt	
		c. Source of funds from which loan made or origin of debt	
		d. Date payment(s) due	
		e. Amount due as of date of commencement	
		f. Current amount due	
		TOTAL: Loans to Others and Accounts Receivable	

J.	12.	Contingent Interests (stock options, interests subject to life estates, prospective inheritances)	
		12.1 a. Description	
		b. Location	
		c. Date of vesting	
		d. Title owner	
		e. Date of acquisition	
		f. Original price or value	
		g. Source of acquisition to acquire	
		h. Method of valuation	
		i. Value as of date of commencement	
		j. Current value	$
		TOTAL: Contingent Interests	$
K.	13.	Other Assets (e.g., tax shelter investments, collections, judgments, causes of action, patents, trademarks, copyrights, and any other asset not hereinabove itemized)	
		13.1 a. Description	
		b. Title owner	

		c. Location	
		d. Original Price or value	
		e. Source of funds to acquire	
		f. Amount of lien unpaid	
		g. Value as of date of commencement	
		h. Current value	
		TOTAL: Other Assets	$
		TOTAL ASSETS:	$

V.		**LIABILITIES**	
A.	1.	Accounts Payable	
		1.1 a. Name and address of creditor	
		b. Debtor	
		c. Amount of original debt	
		d. Date of incurring debt	
		e. Purpose	
		f. Monthly or other periodic payment	
		g. Amount of debt as of date of commencement	
		h. Amount of current debt	
		1.2 a. Name and address of creditor	
		b. Debtor	
		c. Amount of original debt	
		d. Date of incurring debt	
		e. Purpose	
		f. Monthly or other periodic	

		payment	
		g. Amount of debt as of date of commencement	
		h. Amount of current debt	
		TOTAL: Accounts Payable	$
B.		Credit Card Debt	
	2.	2.1 a. Debtor	
		b. Amount of original debt	
		c. Date of incurring debt	
		d. Purpose	
		e. Monthly or other periodic payment	
		f. Amount of debt as of date of commencement	
		g. Amount of current debt	
		2.2 a. Debtor	
		b. Amount of original debt	
		c. Date of incurring debt	
		d. Purpose	
		e. Monthly or other periodic	

		payment	
		f. Amount of debt as of date of commencement	$
		g. Amount of current debt	$
		TOTAL: Credit Card Debt	$
C.	3.	Mortgages Payable on Real Estate	
		3.1 a. Name and address of mortgagee	
		b. Address of property mortgaged	
		c. Mortgagor(s)	
		d. Original debt	
		e. Date of incurring debt	
		f. Monthly or other periodic payment	
		g. Maturity date	
		h. Amount of debt as of date of commencement	
		i. Amount of current debt	
		3.2 a. Name and address of	

		mortgagee	
		b. Address of property mortgaged	
		c. Mortgagor(s)	
		d. Original debt	
		e. Date of incurring debt	
		f. Monthly or other periodic payment	
		g. Maturity date	

		h. Amount of debt as of date of commencement	
		i. Amount of current debt	
		TOTAL: Mortgages Payable	
D.	4.	Home Equity and Other Lines of Credit	
		4.1 a. Name and address of mortgagee	
		b. Address of property mortgaged	
		c. Mortgagor(s)	
		d. Original debt	
		e. Date of incurring debt	
		f. Monthly or other periodic payment	
		g. Maturity date	
		h. Amount of debt at date of commencement	
		i. Amount of current debt	
		TOTAL: Home Equity and Other	$

		Lines of Credit	
E.	5.	Notes Payable	
		5.1 a. Name and address of noteholder	
		b. Debtor	
		c. Amount of original debt	
		d. Date of incurring debt	
		e. Purpose	
		f. Monthly or other periodic payment	
		g. Amount of debt as of date of commencement	
		h. Amount of current debt	
		TOTAL: Notes Payable	$
F.	6.	Brokers Margin Accounts	
		6.1 a. Name and address of broker	
		b. Amount of original debt	
		c. Date of incurring debt	
		d. Purpose	
		e. Monthly or other periodic payment	

		f. Amount of debt as of date of commencement	
		g. Amount of current debt	
		TOTAL: Broker's Margin Accounts	
G.	7.	Taxes Payable	
		7.1 a. Description of Tax	
		b. Amount of Tax	
		c. Date Due	
		TOTAL: Taxes Payable	$
H.	8.	Loans on Life Insurance Policies	
		8.1 a. Name and address of insurer	
		b. Amount of loan	
		c. Date incurred	
		d. Purpose	
		e. Name of Borrower	
		f. Monthly or other periodic payment	
		g. Amount of debt as of date of commencement	
		h. Amount of current debt	

		TOTAL: Loans on Life Insurance	
I.	9.	Installment accounts payable (security agreements, chattel mortgages)	
		9.1 a. Name and address of creditor	
		b. Debtor	
		c. Amount of original debt	
		d. Date of incurring debt	
		e. Purpose	

		f. Monthly or other periodic payment	
		g. Amount of debt as of date of commencement	
		h. Amount of current debt	
		TOTAL: Installment Accounts	$
J.	10.	Other Liabilities	
		10.1 a. Description	
		b. Name and address of creditor	
		c. Debtor	
		d. Original amount of debt	
		e. Date incurred	
		f. Purpose	
		g. Monthly or other periodic payment	
		h. Amount of debt as of date of commencement	
		i. Amount of current debt	
		10.2 a. Description	

		b. Name and address of creditor	
		c. Debtor	
		d. Original amount of debt	
		e. Date incurred	
		f. Purpose	
		g. Monthly or other periodic payment	
		h. Amount of debt as of date of commencement	
		i. Amount of current debt	
		TOTAL: Other Liabilities	$
		TOTAL LIABILITIES	$

VI.   ASSETS TRANSFERRED

List all assets transferred in any manner during the preceding three years, or length of the   marriage, whichever is shorter. Note: Transfers in the routine course of business which   resulted in an exchange of assets of substantially equivalent value need not be specifically   disclosed where such assets are otherwise identified in the Statement of Net Worth.

Description of Property	To Whom Transferred and Relationship to Transferee	Date of Transfer	Value

VII.   LEGAL & EXPERT FEES

Please state the amount you have paid to all lawyers and experts retained in   connection with your marital dissolution, including name of professional, amounts   and dates paid, and source of funds. Attach retainer agreement for your present   attorney.

_____

_____

VIII. OTHER DATA CONCERNING THE FINANCIAL CIRCUMSTANCES OF THE   PARTIES THAT SHOULD BE BROUGHT TO THE ATTENTION OF THE   COURT ARE:

_____

_____

The foregoing statements and a rider consisting of _____ page(s) annexed hereto and made a part hereof, have been carefully read by the undersigned who states that they are true and correct and states same, under oath, subject to the penalties of perjury.

_____

Sworn to before me this
    day of _____, 20_ _   This is the
    _____ Statement of Net Worth

                                           I have filed in

this proceeding.

_____
    Notary Public

                                         Attorney

Certification:

_____

REQUIRED ATTACHMENTS:
    Retainer Agreement
    Most recent W-2, 1099s, K1s and Income Tax Returns

Made in the USA
Columbia, SC
07 January 2019